Copyright © 2020 Hirsch Family

All parts of this book are permitted (and encouraged) to be reproduced, transmitted in any form, photographed via electronic or mechanical means, including photocopying or recording, without prior permission from the publisher, for the sole purpose of spreading Torah.

# Table of Contents

| | |
|---|---|
| Introduction | 6 |
| Parshas Bereishis | 10 |
| Parshas Noach | 14 |
| Parshas Lech Lecho | 17 |
| Parshas Vayeira | 20 |
| Parshas Chayei Sarah | 24 |
| Parshas Toldos | 28 |
| Parshas Vayeitzei | 32 |
| Parshas Vayishlach | 37 |
| Parshas Vayeishev | 42 |
| Parshas Mikeitz | 47 |
| Parshas Vayigash | 50 |
| Parshas Vayechi | 54 |
| Parshas Shemos | 61 |
| Parshas Vaeira | 67 |
| Parshas Bo | 74 |
| Parshas Beshalach | 80 |
| Parshas Yisro | 87 |
| Parshas Mishpatim | 92 |
| Parshas Terumah | 98 |
| Parshas Tetzaveh | 106 |
| Parshas Ki Sisa | 110 |
| Parshas Vayakhel | 115 |

| | |
|---|---|
| Parshas Pekudei | 118 |
| Parshas Vayikra | 121 |
| Parshas Tzav | 126 |
| Parshas Shemini | 130 |
| Parshas Tazria | 135 |
| Parshas Metzorah | 141 |
| Parshas Acharei Mos | 144 |
| Parshas Kedoshim | 148 |
| Parshas Emor | 152 |
| Parshas Behar | 159 |
| Parshas Bechukosai | 163 |
| Parshas Bamidbar | 165 |
| Parshas Naso | 169 |
| Parshas Beha'alosecha | 174 |
| Parshas Shelach | 177 |
| Parshas Korach | 182 |
| Parshas Chukas | 187 |
| Parshas Balak | 193 |
| Parshas Pinchas | 199 |
| Parshas Mattos | 204 |
| Parshas Masai | 208 |
| Parshas Devarim | 214 |
| Parshas Va'eschanan | 218 |
| Parshas Eikev | 223 |
| Parshas Re'eh | 227 |
| Parshas Shoftim | 230 |
| Parshas Ki Tetzei | 234 |

Parshas Ki Savo .................................................................................. 237
Parshas Netzavim ............................................................................. 243
Parshas Vayeilech ............................................................................. 247
Parshas Haazinu ............................................................................... 250
Parshas V'zos HaBracha ................................................................... 252
BIRKAS HAMAZON ....................................................................... 259

# Introduction

To Our Dear Daughter Rochel,

Since you were a young child, we marveled at how alert, receptive, and enthusiastic you were when we would share a Torah thought or concept with you. The amazing part is that, Baruch Hashem and Bli Ayin Harah, it has manifested itself to this day. About a year ago, you decided – on your own – to start emailing weekly Divrei Torah on the Parsha to a group of friends and relatives. Where did this passion and excitement emanate from? Let's see if we can find the answer.

When you were about 6 years old, you may remember that you started learning Parsha through simple original songs, accompanied by short 5 to 10 minute Parsha stories. You listened to them in the car over and over again each week. We were always amazed at how you memorized the songs, singing them months later! Essentially, you learned the basic Parsha story. That was "Level 1."

The following year, after reviewing the basic story, your learning advanced in the form of simple questions and answers. These nuggets of information were reflective of various Divrei Chazal but were used to help elucidate the Parsha narrative. As we went through these questions and answers, we called that "Level 2," since it represented an advancement from the previous year.

The year after that, you moved into a more sophisticated stage of learning, where we discussed one particular Chazal – either a Rashi, Ramban, or Baal HaTurim, for example – and tried to develop observations, thoughts, and ethical lessons. This was "Level 3."

Now let us explain where the concept of these levels originated. When I (Daddy) was in eighth grade, my Rebbe, Rabbi Mordechai Palgon, taught my class various subjects, including Gemara. After he delivered the shiur, he would often offer us an opportunity for growth. For any student who wanted, he provided a little index card that had a written question on it. The index card was marked "Level 2." It represented a question posed by a different commentator, one that we did not cover in class. It fostered curiosity among the students, each of us thinking to ourselves, "Gee, that's a really good question on the Gemara – I wonder what the answer is!" It allowed us to explore and investigate. I myself went and asked many of the older Bais Midrash Bochrim to help me uncover the answers. As I would turn in the card with the answer, Rabbi Palgon always had more – Level 3 and beyond. Each one represented a deeper understanding of the Gemara.

The approach of climbing higher – Level 1, Level 2, Level 3, etc. – was an educational model that created curiosity, excitement, and enthusiasm. That's why we started using it with you. So that you, too, would share that level of enjoyment in Torah learning, with the goal of continuously seeking more.

We are so proud that you have done exactly that, evidenced by your weekly email, where you now share Divrei Torah. We marvel at how you initiated the idea, enthusiastically search for Divrei Torah each week, and self-manage the process! It's beautiful.

Allow us to remind you of a vignette that happened last year. It shows incredible Hashgacha Pratis and also serves as an example of your spiritual progression. In 2019, in reviewing Parshas Terumah, I (Daddy) was learning Artscroll's in-depth translation and elucidation on the Ramban. I was so excited when I found a piece that I thought you would enjoy. I spent time writing down the observations I had on the Ramban and then emailed it to you.

I came home that night very excited and told you to go check your email. Less than 10 minutes later, you came back, holding a print out of a Dvar Torah and said, "Look, Daddy, this is what you wrote a couple years ago." As I started to read the paper, it was the "Level 3" Dvar Torah I had written for you dated in 2017 – over 2 years earlier! Amazingly, it was the exact same Ramban that I had identified earlier that day, with one small difference. The source that I quoted back in 2017 was from an obscure note in the Artscroll Midrash Rabbah, which quoted the same Ramban I had now identified from the source itself!

*Level 3 and Beyond!*

There were two amazing points that came from this: First, I was shocked to see this very same Ramban piqued my interest on *two separate occasions* (two years apart!) from *two different Sefarim*!

Second, I asked you how you remembered what I had written from 2017 in mere minutes, after reading the Dvar Torah that I had emailed you that day. You explained that earlier in the week, you knew you had to prepare and deliver a Dvar Torah in school, so you were looking through your old Parsha notebooks and found that Dvar Torah from 2017. So when you read my email that night in 2019, the one from two years earlier was already fresh in your mind!

The fact that you went back to your Parsha notebook – on your own – to review what you had learned years earlier spoke volumes. It showed your diligence. It evidenced your enthusiasm. It displayed your love for learning Torah. But more importantly than anything else, it symbolized your growth pattern.

So what's inside the Sefer you are holding in your hand? Your journey of growth. Each Parsha starts off with the original song composed for you, back in 2013 and 2014. This is, in essence, "Level 1." Then, in subsequent years, there are Divrei Torah adapted from reputable Rabbeim and Sefarim (sources are cited to give appropriate credit). Many of these formed your "Level 2," sprinkling nuggets of interesting Torah thoughts into the basic Parsha narrative. Finally, the remaining Divrei Torah in this Sefer originated from personal observations on a Chazal shared with you, along with some observations that you developed on your own through our learning discussions. These are the "Level 3" Divrei Torah.

As you flip through this Sefer, you will notice an incredible upward trend between 2013 and 2019, with the level of sophistication increasing exponentially over the years. You should use this as a motivation for what you can accomplish as you keep advancing spiritual levels for the rest of your life!

But regardless of the sources and content, there are two common denominators that flow throughout this Sefer – time our family spent together and your spiritual growth. You sang these Parsha songs while driving around with Mommy. You learned Divrei

Torah on Friday's with Daddy. You spoke these words of Torah at the Shabbos table. This Sefer is much more than a compilation of Torah thoughts – it is a treasure trove of time our family spent together and your growth through the process. Not just learning Torah, but in developing a relationship. The time we spend together is precious and we should never take it for granted.

Amazingly enough, this Sefer is only a small fraction of your growth pattern. Aside from your school curriculum, you have studied the Yahadus series (getting halfway through volume 1 still counts!), the biography of the Chofetz Chaim, the biography of Sarah Schenirer, Living Emunah for Teens, and most recently, the biography of Rebbetzin Kanievsky. You don't just read these Sefarim. You take notes summarizing what you learn. You discuss the lesson. You constantly want to learn more. And the lessons have become a part of you. This is spiritual growth and we celebrate together with you.

This concept of growth, spending time together, and building a relationship doesn't stop with our family. The way you develop your relationship with Hashem is also by spending time with Him – through learning Torah, davening, performing Mitzvos, and loving Chesed. Always remember that the relationship we developed serves as the model for how you will continuously strengthen your relationship, and grow closer to, Hashem.

As you embark into the stage of a Bas Mitzvah, you have the opportunity to continuously climb higher! Level 3 is only one notch on Hashem's ladder that has unlimited rungs. It is our hope and Bracha that you always cherish your love for learning – and use this Sefer as a motivation to "go beyond" in your spiritual growth.

Mazel Tov!

Mommy and Daddy

# Parshas Bereishis

## I. 2013 (Song)

*(Tune of "Ki-Metzion")*

Simchas Torah, lots of dancing, all boys and girls are excited.
The last Parsha, called "Zos HaBracha," makes all of us delighted.

It's when we go, on the shoulders, of our very own daddy.
We hop around, sing and dance because we're so happy.

The lesson we learn, on this day, is to love the Torah,
Live it and breathe it, love it and sneeze it, learn it from your Mora.

Take it with you on an airplane, always have it in your brain,
Because it's about, Hashem knowing, you're always going to gain.

## II. 2016 (Part 1)

**Question:** Why doesn't the Torah start with the first Mitzvah given to the Jewish people (Rosh Chodesh)? Rashi explains it had to start with the Creation of the world so that if anyone claimed Israel does not belong to the Jews, we could explain that Hashem created the world and HE gets to decide who receives which land. But Rashi doesn't explain why the Torah had to continue with the remainder of the narrative in Sefer Bereishis! What is the point of all the rest of Sefer Bereishis and why couldn't the Torah then discuss the first Mitzvah?

**Answer:** All of the stories in Sefer Bereishis contain vital lessons in Middos. The stories of Kayin/Hevel, Noach, Avraham, Yitzchak, Yaakov, and Yosef all have the lessons of Middos! The Torah is telling us that you must have a strong foundation in Middos even BEFORE you start doing the Mitzvos!

**Source:** Living with the Parsha, page 12

## III. 2016 (Part 2)

**Question:** Each day, Hashem said "Tov," but on Friday, Hashem says "VERY good." Why only on Friday?

**Answer #1:** Each day was seperate but when all the living creations do their job together – and that could only happen after everything was created on Friday – Hashem was very pleased because of the teamwork performed by all creations!

**Answer #2:** The whole purpose of creation was man. The goal is for man to appreciate what Hashem made for him and to recognize that Hashem controls the world. Indeed, the word "Meod – very" in Hebrew has the same letters as "Adam," indicating that it was only "Meod" because of what "Adam" could now recognize on the sixth day of creation!

**Source:** Rav Dovid Feinstein in "Seasonings of the Torah," page 29

## IV. 2016 (Part 3)

**Question:** If the trees/vegetation were created on the third day, why didn't it sprout until Friday?

**Answer:** Hashem was waiting for someone to appreciate the rain. Only when man was made on the sixth day could someone appreciate the rain. This shows the importance of appreciation.
**Source:** Let There Be Rain by Rabbi Wallerstein

# V. 2016 (Part 4)

**Question:** While the commentaries speculate on what type of tree the Eitz Hadas was, the Torah does not specifically mention it. Why not?

**Answer:** Hashem didn't want to embarrass it, as people would forever say, "This is the tree that caused so much pain to the world. If Hashem didn't want to embarrass a tree, how much more so we should be careful not to embarrass other people!

**Source:** Love Your Neighbor by Rabbi Pliskin

# VI. 2016 (Part 5)

**Question:** Hashem said, "Let us make a man." We all know that there is only one Hashem. Why, then, is this written in the plural?

**Answer:** Rashi notes that while Hashem obviously didn't need any help creating man, He discussed this with the angels in heaven, in order to teach us Derech Eretz, respect for the opinion of others and the value of humility (i.e., no one should feel that they are so great that they need not discuss their problems with others). As Rabbi Elchonon Wasserman, z'tl taught, from here "we see how important it is for the Jew to be an individual of good character, to be humble and friendly."

**Lesson:** This could also be a contributing reason to why we say Derech Eretz Kadma LaTorah – that Derech Eretz comes even BEFORE learning the Torah!

**Source:** http://www.anshe.org/parsha/bereshis.htm

# VII. 2017 (Part 1)

**Question:** The Sofei Teivos (last letters) of the words "Bereishis Barah Elokim" is "Emes," showing that the world was created with truth. If so, why is this hinted using the last letters of each word? Why not make it the Roshei Teivos (first letters of each word)?

**Answer:** Because we don't see the whole truth until the very "end" of the story.

**Source:** Power of a Vort by Rabbi Frand

# VIII. 2017 (Part 2)

**Background:** The Yalkut explains that the Torah starts off with the letter "Beis" because it stands for "Bracha – blessing." However, the Zera Shimshon notes that in Tehillim (119:160), we say to Hashem, "Your very first utterance is Emes, truth." If so, why didn't the Torah start off with an Alef, referring to the word, "Emes – truth?"

**Answer:** The Zera Shimshon explains that Hashem's blessings are not automatic. However, the Torah is telling how to earn those Brachos, and that is by acting honestly, with Emes. This is alluded in the final letters of each of the words "...Barah Elokim Es...," which spell "Emes." Meaning to say, you can read the first verse in the Torah, "In the beginning, the very first thing is...Emes!" With the importance of Emes hinted in the very first posuk, the Torah wanted to emphasize that Brachos (the "Beis") will only come when a person acts with honesty!

**Lesson:** Being honest and truthful will lead a person to receive all the blessings Hashem has to offer!
**Source:** Zera Shimshon, Artscroll Volume 1

# Parshas Noach

## I. 2013 (Song)

*(tune of "Ben Digamos")*

Parshas Noach is about a man,
Who Hashem told His plan,
To build a huge boat called an ark,
To carry him, his family, and all animals in the park.

Rain fell all 40 days and nights,
And it showed Hashem's might,
At the end of the rainstorm,
A raven and dove were sent to inform.

Flooding the world will never happen again,
Rainbows are the promise to men,
The lesson we learn from Noach,
Is to listen to Hashem with Koach.

## II. 2014

**Question:** Noach had to bring in 7 pairs of each Kosher animal and one pair of non-Kosher animals. Some say there were 300 rooms, others say 900 rooms on the ark. Plus there was a year's worth of food. How was there room for every animal?

**Answer:** There wasn't enough room, Hashem made a miracle, but ONLY after Noach did his Hishtadlus (efforts) by building it the best way he could.

**Lesson:** You have to make your best effort, and then Hashem will take it from there. (Little Midrash Says, page 61)

## III. 2015

**Question:** What else did Noach bring into the Teiva besides animals?

**Answer:** Rashi explains he brought in all the fruits of the world.

**Our Observation:** All the animals of the world came to Noach. He didn't have to go anywhere to get them. But for the fruits, Noach had to venture all over the world to gather the fruits together. This shows his commitment to listening to the word of Hashem!

## IV. 2016

**Question:** Noach was ordered to build a "Tzohar" on top of the Ark. Rashi says there are two opinions as to what the Tzohar was – either a bright gem or a window. According to the opinion that it was a window, why would Hashem want Noach to build a window?

**Answer #1:** Hashem wanted Noach to feel the pain when he saw all the people drowning in the flood.

**Answer #2:** So that Noach could see the Heavens and it would remind Noach that Hashem was watching over the Teiva!

**Lesson:** Based on the first answer, you should always feel other people's pain.

**Source:** Rabbi Shalom Rosner's Parsha shiur, 5776, quoting the Shalhevet Yosef and Gemara in Brachos

*Level 3 and Beyond!*

# V. 2017

**Background:** Rashi explains (7:4) that Hashem delayed the flood by 7 additional days in order for the people of the generation to mourn for the passing of Mesushelach, Noach's grandfather, who was known to be a great Tzadik. In order to properly give him the respect that he deserved, Hashem pushed off the flood for 7 days so that the people could properly mourn for him.

**Question:** Let's consider this generation. They were guilty of idol worship, immorality, and stealing. They even said that if they saw Noach entering the Ark, they would break it and kill Noach (see Rashi to 7:13). How could it be that these people – who had sunk so low – were going to show proper respect to Mesushelach, worthy enough of delaying the flood by 7 days?

**Our Suggested Answer:** No matter how far a person has fallen, one has the capability of rising above and acting properly. Despite the generation's terrible behavior, they were able to dig deep into their Neshamos and ignite the spark that allowed them to show proper respect to a Tzadik.

**Lesson:** We have to realize how capable we really are. No matter how many mistakes we make, we are always able to rise above and act like a mentch. Additionally, we should never lose hope in anyone else, realizing that they, too, have the ability to act like a mentch if they put their mind to it!

# Parshas Lech Lecho

## I. 2013 (Song)

*(tune of "Twinkle Twinkle Little Star")*

This week's Parsha is Lech Lecho,
Hashem told Avraham several new laws.

Idols and bad guys must be gone,
Go to the land of Eretz Canaan.

Avraham and Lot had a fight,
Lot went to evil Sodom that very night.

Hashem told Avraham the stars in the sky,
Will be like your many children – nobody can deny.

Avraham gave himself a bris,
Hashem promises we will live in bliss.

## II. 2014

**Question:** After Lot had a fight with Avraham, he went to Sodom because he thought he was going to get rich. What were Lot's mistakes?

**Answer:** He made two mistakes: (1) He left a Tzadik (Avraham) who was a good influence on him and (2) He went to live with people who were a bad influence on him.

**Lesson:** No matter how much money you hope to make, the first priority has to be the friends and the positive influences around you.

**Source:** Little Midrash Says, page 71

# III. 2016

**Question:** Avraham was scared of having his bris because he was 99 years old. Hashem said that He would do it with him by holding Avraham's hand. Why didn't Hashem just do it for him?

**Answer:** Hashem wanted to teach the lesson that when you are scared, do your Hishtadlus and then Hashem will help you by doing it with you.

**Rochel's Observation:** If Hashem did it for him, then Avraham wouldn't have had a part in the Mitzvah of Bris Milah. Of course, Hashem wants you to get credit for doing the Mitzvah yourself!

**Lesson:** Always do your Hishtadlus!

**Source:** Rashi and Rabbi Zecharya Wallerstein (based on a shiur given on November 8, 2016)

# IV. 2017

**Background:** After Avraham and Lot separated (because of the fight they had regarding where the animals would graze), the Torah stresses that Hashem spoke to Avraham only after Lot moved away. Rashi (13:14) explains that this is because Hashem had distanced Himself from Avraham when Lot was present because Lot was considered to be a Rasha.

**Question #1:** Why should Avraham be excommunicated from Hashem just because Lot was around? Didn't Avram's greatness outweigh any negative vibes from Lot?

**Question #2:** Avraham was the one who taught everyone that there was a Creator. He would even encourage people to bentch after eating by not charging them on the condition that they thanked Hashem for the food. If Avraham was used to being around people who didn't recognize a Creator – and he was constantly trying to teach people about Hashem – why wouldn't Hashem talk to Avraham just because of Lot being around?

**Our Suggested Answer:** The power of a negative influence is much stronger than we realize. It's one thing when the people were ignorant and were being educated by Avraham. But it's a whole different level when a person is wicked and a Rasha. Such a person brings a bad atmosphere wherever they go, to the extent that even Hashem doesn't want to be in their presence. If Hashem refused to be in the presence of a wicked person, all the more so we should be careful not to be around people who are negative influences.

**Lesson:** The people we keep around us have a tremendous influence on us!

# Parshas Vayeira

## I. 2013 (Song)

*(tune of "This Old Man...")*

This week's Parsha is Vayeira,
Three angels visited Avraham and Sarah,
Hachnasas Orchim was done for them,
The angels said they would get a gem.

The people of Sodom were very mean,
Hashem sent fire to make Sodom clean,
Sarah had a baby, it was a Neis,
His name was Yitzchak and full of grace,

Hashem asked Avraham, to sacrifice his son,
But the angel told him no, and that he had won.
The lesson we learn from this event,
Is to trust Hashem and be content.

## II. 2014

**Question:** Avraham did tremendous Chesed for all his three guests when they came to visit: He got them bread, milk, and then meat. Almost everything was done with excitement, enthusiasm, and in excess, solely for the benefit of his guests. The only exception was that when Avraham offered the men water, he specified getting them "a little" water. Why did Avraham suddenly seem to get stingy?

**Answer:** The Lekach Tov explains that the water was the only item he needed others to help him get; all other items he took care of himself. This act shows Avraham's sensitivity to others even MORE because the water was the only item that Avraham didn't have time to fetch himself. Avraham's thinking was that if he was going to trouble his servants to get the water, he had no right to ask them to bring more water than is actually needed. It was Avraham's sensitivity to his staff that compelled him to only offer a small quantity of water to his guests.

**Lesson:** We, too, need to be mindful of the needs of those around us, especially our family and friends, and take no one for granted.

**Source:** Weekly Dvar by Shlomo Ressler

# III. 2016

**Question:** The Torah tells us all of the details about Avraham's Hachnasas Orchim. For example, the Torah tells us that Avraham ran to greet the guests, got them milk and meat, and a basket to wash their feet and hands. Why does the Torah go into such detail about what Avraham did? It could have just said he welcomed the guests!

**Answer:** The Torah is teaching us that each detail is a big part of the Mitzvah of Hachnasas Orchim.

**Lesson:** When we have guests/visitors, we should do Hachnasas Orchim with lots of Zerizus, Kavannah, and details. For example, when new visitors come in, say "Welcome," offer them a tour around your house, and give them good and drinks!

**Source:** Growth through Torah, page 45

# IV. 2017

**Question:** Why did Lot merit to be saved from the destruction of Sodom?

*Level 3 and Beyond!* 21

**Answer:** Rashi explains (19:29) that when Sarah was taken by Pharaoh in Egypt, Lot heard Avraham say that Sarah was his sister. Although Lot knew that Avraham and Sarah were actually husband and wife, he did not reveal this information to Pharaoh. Since Lot went out of his way for Avraham, he merited that Hashem went out of his way for Lot and saved him from the destruction of Sodom.

**Our Question #1:** Lot didn't have to do anything special. He just had to keep quiet! Why should a simple act of keeping quiet yield the reward of being saved from Sodom?

**Our Question #2:** While Lot may have become rich by revealing the true relationship between Avraham and Sarah – and thereby falling into the good graces of Pharaoh who may have made him rich – such an act would have jeopardized his uncle's life. Although tempted by the money, any rational person would have done the same thing and chosen their family's life over riches. Why was Lot rewarded in such a grandiose manner for an act that appears to be something any rational person would do?

**Our Suggested Answer #1:** Keeping quiet is harder than we think! Whether it's money or any other incentives, human nature is to talk and reveal things when we should remain quiet. Since it is so hard to do, Hashem gave Lot an amazing reward – one that saved his life – by keeping quiet at a time when he was greatly tempted to talk!

**Our Suggested Answer #2:** Even if we were to say that Lot's actions were small and easy to do, it would teach us that even the small actions can make a big difference. Perhaps Hashem is teaching us that even the small acts – like keeping quiet – can have large ramifications, including being saved from the destruction of Sodom!

**Lesson:** Keeping quiet is hard to do, but if we control ourselves and keep quiet when we know we should, Hashem will give us incredible rewards! Additionally, even if it may seem easy for us to hold back, we should understand how Hashem gives great rewards for even small actions.

## V. 2018

**Question:** If Avraham was so anxious to be hospitable and gracious to his guests, why did he only offer them a little bit of water for their feet, recline against the tree, and a morsel of bread? Why not give them buckets of water to wash their whole body, beds to sleep inside a tent, and plenty of bread to satiate them?

**Answer:** The Ramban says in 18:3 that Avraham saw they were traveling on the road to their destination and would not want to spend the night. They would not want to be delayed in their traveling, so Avraham offered them only what they absolutely needed, but not an excessive amount that would delay them.

**Our Observation & Possible Homiletic Lesson:** Perhaps this is a good Mashal for life: Very often, we don't get an abundance; but just enough to get by. Perhaps Hashem is telling us, "You are getting exactly what you need because if I give you an abundance, it will delay and distract you from your mission." So getting the bare minimum of what we need might actually be a great sign from Hashem that we are traveling on the road in a proper manner towards our mission!

# Parshas Chayei Sarah

## I. 2013 (Song)

*(tune of "Oh Susanna")*

Chayei Sarah starts with Sarah living with Hashem,
Avraham was sad but found a place to bury his precious gem,
Maras HaMachpela was how it was known,
It was 400 shekalim and he bought it from Efron.

Avraham told Eliezer that Yitzchak needed a wife,
To go and find a woman who did Chesed with her life.
A girl named Rivkah was standing at a well,
She offered water to him and his camels.

Chesed and Middos were Rivkah's special traits,
She married Yitzchak and they were very happy mates.
The lesson that we learn is to always be kind,
Have Chesed and other people always on your mind.

## II. 2014

**Question:** Why did Avraham tell Eliezer to go to Aram (his birthplace) instead of Canaan (where they were living)? Both places served idols; what was better about one from the other?

**Answer:** In Aram, they were nice to each other with good Middos, whereas in Canaan they were not.

# III. 2015

**Question:** Eliezer approaches Rivkah, who had just filled her pitcher with water, and asks if he could drink. She graciously gives him some water from her pitcher, and then offers to provide water for his camels. Rivkah returned to the well, drew water and poured it into the trough for Eliezer's camels. The Midrash comments that Eliezer approached Rivkah because he noticed something miraculous occurring when she approached the well: the water rose to greet her. Eliezer realized that this was no ordinary young woman, and so he decided to approach her and see if she would offer water for his camels. Rav Levi Yitzchak of Berdichev noted that although the water in the well rose to greet Rivkah, she had to work hard to draw water for Eliezer's camels. Apparently, the water that had initially risen went back down into the well. Why did it go down and make it harder for Rivkah?

**Answer:** The reason is that the true value of a Mitzvah is the effort and hard work invested in it. Once Rivkah decided to do the Mitzvah of drawing water for the visitor's camels, Hashem sent the water back down so she would have to work to fulfill the Mitzvah.

**Lesson:** When you work hard for something, that's how you know what's truly important to that person! Anyone can do an "easy" Chesed, but when you do a "hard" Chesed and it's a lot of work, it says a lot about who you are!

**Source:** Rabbi Eli Mansour

# IV. 2016

**Question:** What can we learn from the way Avraham acted towards Efron?

**Answer:** Even if you're in a very bad situation, you should always have Derech Eretz and always make a Kiddush Hashem. Just think, Avraham lost his wife, he almost had to give up his son as a sacrifice (to Hashem), had to kick out his son Yishmael from his house, and Hashem gave him 10 tests! Avraham could have gotten upset with Efron for charging him 400 shekalim, but instead, Avraham acted nicely and with Derech Eretz.

**Lesson:** Even when you're having a really bad day, you still have to act with Derech Eretz.

**Source:** Michtav MeEliyahu

## V. 2017

**Question:** Eliezer was waiting to see which woman would offer him and his camels water before determining who was the right girl for Yitzchak. However, the Torah is very specific when mentioning that Eliezer waited until the camels finished drinking before he concluded Rivkah was the right girl. Why did he have to wait until the camels finished drinking? Why not conclude that Rivkah was the right one as soon as she offered water for them to drink?

**Answer:** The Zera Shimon explains, based on a Midrash Rabbah (60:8) that the camels that were with Eliezer were very special. These camels were the type of animals that would normally not eat from another person's field if it didn't belong to their master (e.g., Avraham). Therefore, Eliezer waited for these camels to actually drink the water – because he knew that Avraham's special camels, who inherently had this special sensitivity, would not lead him in the wrong direction! Eliezer concluded that if the camels completed drinking it, then he knew Rivkah was the proper girl for Yitzchak.

**Our Question:** The camels played an integral role in choosing Yitzchak's mate. Eliezer relied on them heavily to make the right decision, proving just how special these camels were. How did the camels develop such a sensitivity and become so special?

**Our Suggested Answer:** There could be several possibilities, including: (a) the way that a Tzadik acts influences even his animals or (b) in the merit of Avraham acting so holy, Hashem gave him special animals. Regardless of the manner in which the animals became special, the bottom line is that Avraham had sensitive and caring camels, and it wasn't by coincidence. If a person can either influence or have the merit to have caring animals based on the way he acts, all the more so a person will have caring and sensitive human beings (e.g., family and friends) just by acting like a Mentch!

**Lesson:** If we want to be surrounded by people who are loving, caring, and sensitive, we have to make sure we act that way first, and then the rest will follow!

**Source:** Zera Shimshon, Artscroll Volume 1

# Parshas Toldos

## I. 2013 (Song)

*(tune of "The Bear went Over the Mountain")*

Toldos is a Parsha, where Rivkah had twin children,
They were very different, different types of men.

Yaakov learned Torah, from his Morah,
Eisav was bad news; he sold his Bechor for lentil soup,
Yitzchak gave a Bracha to Yaakov instead of Eisav.

Rivkah knew Eisav was very very tough,
He would hurt his brother, which is bad for the mother,
She told Yaakov to ruuuuuun to Padan Aram.

The lesson we learn from Yaakov is to be a Yeled Tov
To be a Yeled Tov, to be a Yeled Tov.
And then Hashem will give us Rov [means plentiful]!!

## II. 2014 (Part 1)

**Question:** What is the one Mitzvah we can learn from Eisav?

**Answer:** Kibud Av Va'eim – honoring your parents. Eisav did this Mitzvah extremely well by: (1) Bringing his father Yitzchak a new animal to eat every night and (2) putting on his nice clothing when bringing his father dinner (not his normal animal hunting suit).

# III. 2014 (Part 2)

**Question:** Rashi says that when Rivkah passed by the Yeshiva of Shem and Ever, Yaakov wanted to come out, but when she passed by a house of idol worship, Eisav wanted to come out. Knowing that an angel teaches the person all of the Torah while still in the womb, we can understand why Eisav would have wanted to come out, but why would Yaakov want to leave, especially when he is learning Torah directly from an angel?

**Answer:** Rabbi Chaim Solovechik of Brisk explains that if a person is next to an evil person, like Eisav, it is better to get away from the bad influence, even if it means giving up learning with an angel!

**Lesson:** This is a lesson on making sure we surround ourselves with good people!

**Source:** Growth Through Torah, page 61

# IV. 2016

**Question:** When Rivkah was having the war inside her womb (between Yaakov and Eisav), she wasn't sure what was happening. Rashi says she went to Shem (the Navi) to inquire for help. Why did Rivkah go to Shem and not directly to Hashem to ask for help?

**Answer:** The Chasam Sofer explains that Shem (a true Tzadik) was considered like the head of the body, while the Jewish people were considered like the rest of the body. And of course, the head is allowed to daven for other parts of the body! The Jewish people are all one unit. When a person feels the pain of another as if it were himself, they are considered like one. Therefore, Rivkah was asking

*Level 3 and Beyond!*

Shem to help figure it out, but of course, she was still looking to Hashem!

**Lesson:** We should always feel another person's pain as if it were our own.

**Source:** Chasam Sofer, quoted by http://torah24-7.com/video/Toldot-Why-is-it-ok-to-ask-a-tz

# V. 2017

**Background:** When Yitzchak marries Rivkah, the posuk goes out of its way to say that Rivkah was the daughter of Besuel, the sister of Lavan, and from the place of Padan Aram. Rashi (25:20) explains that the reason the Torah repeats each of these biographical details is to emphasize how great she was that she did not learn the evil ways of her wicked father, brother, and neighbors from where she came from.

**Question #1:** Rivkah was only three years old when she married Yitzchak. The time she would have been around these wicked people would have been very limited, especially when considering that a good portion of the time she would have been an infant. Why does the Torah laud her with praise that she did not learn from their evil ways when her exposure to them was minuscule?

**Question #2:** Rivkah being influenced by her wicked father and brother is understandable, as she was living under the same roof as them. However, regarding the city she was from (Padan Aram), Rashi clearly states that she was from a place of wicked people – but it appears from Rashi's words that there was no deeper relationship. Notice that Rashi did not say she was friends or colleagues with them – only that she was from the same place. What influence could wicked people have if Rivkah didn't have a relationship with any of them?

**Our Suggested Answer:** From the words of Rashi, it is clear that Rivkah's surroundings – no matter how limited in time, scope, or depth – could have had a profound impact on her. Her fortitude and perseverance in not allowing her wicked father and brother to influence her – despite it being for a short period of time – was a noteworthy attribute. Further, the mere presence of living in a city surrounded by wicked people, even though she had no meaningful relationship with them, could have obstructed her spiritual growth. The fact that she did not allow any of these factors to influence her was worthy of the Torah repeating her biographical details, showing how hard she worked to remain committed to a Torah lifestyle.

**Lesson:** We see how strong bad influences can be, even for short periods of time and even without depth to the relationship. The opposite is also true: if we attach ourselves to people committed to Torah, we will gain exponentially!

# Parshas Vayeitzei

## I. 2013 (Song)

*(tune of "Mode Ani")*

This week's Parsha is Vayeitzei,
Yaakov created Maariv to pray,
He went to sleep,
And had a dream that mattered,
About angels going up and down a ladder.

*(tune of "we wash our yadayim, three times it's true...")*

Yaakov worked for 7 years,
Lavan tricked him and gave him Leah with tears.
Yaakov worked again because he knew,
Rochel was the one he really wanted, too.

*(back to "Mode Ani")*

Yaakov had four beautiful wives,
Altogether, they had 12 tribes,
The lesson we learn from Yaakov's years of work,
Is to be honest, truthful, and just smirk.

## II. 2014

**Background:** The posuk describes the deceitful incident in which Lavan switched daughters on Yaakov Avinu, giving him Leah as a bride instead of Rochel. The posuk says, "And it was in the morning, and behold it was Leah!" [Bereishis 29:25]. Rashi elaborates: "But at night Yaakov assumed that she was not Leah because he had given signs to Rochel by which she could identify herself to him. However, when Rochel saw they were taking Leah to him, she said "Now my sister will be humiliated." She therefore arose and gave her those signs."

**Midrash**: The Midrash [Pesikta Rabasi to Sefer Eichah] tells us that when Klal Yisrael was banished from Israel and was headed toward the Babylonian exile, every one of our ancestors came to petition Hashem that He should have mercy on the Jewish people and end the exile. The Midrash provides a whole list of people including Avraham, Yitzchak, Yaakov, and Moshe, who each offered prayers to Heaven beseeching Divine mercy in the merit of acts of righteousness they performed during their lifetime. Hashem responded in the negative to each of them! Finally, Rochel came and invoked her sacrifice of being willing to give up the husband she loved, to spare the embarrassment of her sister on her wedding night. She asked that Hashem grant mercy to the Jewish people in the merit of that act. The Midrash relates that when Rochel recalled this ultimate sacrifice on her part, Hashem's mercy was aroused and Hashem promised that because of Rochel's Chesed, Hashem would bring an end to the exile.

**Question**: How can one compare Rochel's action to Akeidas Yitzchak – sacrificing one's own son or a willingness to be sacrificed? Yet we see Rochel's action trumped the Avos and Moshe. Why?

**Answer**: This is the power of true Chesed, where Rochel didn't just give up something at this moment, but it could have affected the rest of her life. She did this Chesed without reservations or hesitation – all to save her sister the embarrassment.

**Lesson**: This is how important wholehearted Chesed is and the power it can have.

**Source**: Rabbi Frand

## III. 2015

**Question:** Yaakov has a dream, where he sees angels walking up and down the ladder that extended from the earth to the Heavens. What does the ladder represent?

**Answer:** The "Ladder" is that of prayer. The Gematria (numerical value) of the Hebrew words for "ladder" and "voice" are equivalent. From this we learn an interesting symbolism – just as the ladder in Yaakov's dream connected the earth to heaven allowing the angels to ascend and descend on it, so do our voices (i.e., our prayers) connect us to heaven.

**Lesson:** Our davening is more than just lip service – it is what connects us to Hashem!

**Source:** Kol Dodi on the Torah (Rabbi David Feinstein)

## IV. 2016

**Background:** When Yaakov went to sleep, the rocks were fighting over who was going to be the pillow for Yaakov under his head, since they all wanted to be under the head of a Tzadik. So Hashem made a miracle and made ALL the rocks become one big rock!

**Question:** If Hashem was making a miracle anyway, then why didn't he make them a comfortable pillow instead of one big rock?

**Answer:** the Vilna Gaon says this was to teach us an important lesson about fighting. The message is that nothing comfortable ever comes from fighting, even when it is for a good reason, like being under the head of a Tzadik.

**Lesson:** Fighting is not good, EVEN if you think it is for a good reason!

**Source:** Vila Gaon, cited by http://www.torah24-7.com/video/Vayetze-Why-didn-t-the-stones-t

# V. 2017

**Background:** The pesukim tell us that when Hashem saw Leah was unloved, Hashem opened her womb and gave Leah children. Rochel was then "jealous" of Leah and said to Yaakov, "Give me children, and if not, I am dead." (see the pesukim to 29:31-30:1)

**Question #1:** What is the connection between Hashem seeing that Leah was unloved and therefore giving her children?

**Question #2:** How can we say that Rochel was "jealous" of Leah – wasn't Rochel on an incredibly high spiritual level and above petty jealousy?

**Answer:** The Zera Shimshon explains this by quoting the Gemara that says (Yevamos 64a) the reason why our forefathers were barren and did not have children is because Hashem wants the davening of the holy Tzadikim. Yaakov erroneously believed that it was not the husband's responsibility to daven for their wives. But he was about to learn otherwise. Based on this Gemara, the Zera Shimshon explains the following chain reaction of events:

- Hashem realized that if Yaakov was going to daven for any of his wives, it would have been Rochel because she was the main matriarch in the house, whom he initially wanted to marry. Therefore, since Hashem saw Leah was "unloved," Hashem decided to open her womb first since Yaakov would not be davening for her anyway.

*Level 3 and Beyond!* 35

- As a result of Leah giving birth without Yaakov davening, Yaakov thought that since Leah had children without any of his Tefillos, therefore it is not necessary for Yaakov to daven for his wives to have children.
- As a result of seeing that Leah had children without Yaakov davening, Rochel thought that the only reason Leah had children was out of pure merits. This made Rochel jealous that Leah had accumulated more merits through Torah and Mitzvos (which is the only thing a person is allowed to be jealous of!), realizing that she did not have those merits!
- As a result of Rochel realizing she had no merits, Rochel, therefore, told Yaakov that his presumption was wrong and that he needed to daven for her. Without merits, she would be considered "dead" because any person lacking Torah and Mitzvos is not worth living! So she was correcting his erroneous thinking and telling him that he did indeed have to daven for her!

**Lesson:** We see that when a person is lacking something, oftentimes it could be that Hashem desires the Tefillos of that person. After all, the whole point of Tefilla is to connect with Hashem, so if Hashem doesn't give it to you quickly, it may be an indication that you need to better "connect" to Hashem and only THEN He will give it to you!

**Source:** Zera Shimshon, Artscroll Volume 1

# Parshas Vayishlach

## I. 2013 (Song)

*(tune of "I'm a Little Tea Pot")*

Parshas Vayishlach is about,
Eisav and 400 men en route,
They wanted to hurt Yaakov's offspring,
Yaakov did three things: davening, presents, and preparing.

Later that night, there was a fight,
Between Yaakov and Eisav's angel, who had great might.
Yaakov won with Hashem's help,
Then Eisav came and didn't even yelp.

Dina was taken by a very bad prince,
But her brothers, Shimon and Levi, saved her since,
Rochel went to live with Hashem,
A place by the name of Beis Lechem.

The lesson that we learn from Yaakov's behavior,
Don't get angry and know Hashem is our savior.

## II. 2015

**Question:** When Eisav and Yaakov greeted each other, each described their material status in the world. Eisav said, (Bereishis 33:9), "I have a lot." Yaakov said, (Bereishis 33:11), "I have everything." What does this say about their personalities?

**Answer:** These are the two opposing perspectives of Yaakov and Eisav. Eisav lives only for the material world. One's material desires

*Level 3 and Beyond!*

are never satisfied. No matter how much one has, he always wants more. Therefore, Eisav describes his financial position as "I have a lot." Rashi says, "Much more than I need." Nevertheless, I want more. Yaakov, on the other hand, focuses on the spiritual world. He is happy with his material possessions because they are only a means to an end and not an end in themselves. His necessities are fulfilled.

**Mashal**: Rav Eliyohu Lopian tells the following parable to illustrate the concept of having everything you need. A certain man once bragged to his friend about the expensive merchandise that he owned. "What sort of merchandise is it?" the friend asked. The man led him to a cabinet full of expensive medicines. He explained that the doctor had told him to take these medicines. They were very expensive, and very rare, imported from all over the world. The entire time that the owner was bragging about his medicine collection, his friend was thinking, "How fortunate am I that I don't need all of this." Although people are naturally jealous of other's possessions, no one would be jealous of having all of these medicines.

**Lesson:** We have to know that Hashem gives us everything we need. Not one thing is missing. He gives us all of the food, clothing, treats, playing time, books, and toys that we need. We may want more. We may want what other kids have. We may think that we need it. If we needed that thing, Hashem would have given it to us because He gives us all that we need. As Yaakov Avinu said, "I have everything." Everything that I need.

**Source:** http://ohr.edu/youth/kinder/5759/bereishi/vayishla.htm

# III. 2016

**Background:** Eisav's angel attacked Yaakov when He went back to get the little jugs from across the Yabok river.

**Question:** Why did Eisav's angel attack Yaakov specifically at that time? Why not any other time?

**Answer:** Rav Yaakov Kamenetzky explains that when Yaakov went to go get the little jars, he was alone and without his family. When a person is alone, they are not as protected from the Yetzer Harah and the Satan. But when a person is with people who are good influences and who learn Torah/do Mitzvos, they are more protected. Therefore, Eisav's angel attacked Yaakov when he was alone and less protected.

**Lesson:** Always be around good influences.

**Rochel's Observation:** Perhaps another reason why the angel attacked Yaakov at that time is because Hashem was being sensitive to Yaakov's family. If they saw him being attacked, they would have been worried. This way, they didn't see or know about it until later.

**Source:** Rabbi Frand in "The Power of a Vort," page 66-68

# IV. 2017

**Background:** After Eisav meets Yaakov with his 400 men, the encounter ends when Eisav goes back to Seir. When Eisav leaves, Rashi (33:16) explains that he went back alone since each of the 400 men, one by one, abandoned him. Rashi continues that for the wise decision of leaving Eisav, their descendants were rewarded by being saved from an attack of Dovid HaMelech when Dovid was trying to eradicate the Amalekim. During that attack, 400 men escaped, as a reward for their ancestors' act of parting ways with Eisav.

**Observation #1:** The 400 men who left Eisav did not do so out of pure intentions. The Yefeh Toar on the Bereishis Rabbah (78:15) explains that when they saw Eisav trying to bite Yaakov, the 400 men were afraid Eisav was going to go to war with Yaakov and they did not want to do so and immediately left! Despite this lack of pure motives, Hashem still repaid their descendants with a reward! (See Artscroll Rashi, note #3 to 33:16)

**Observation #2:** Eisav's henchmen were evil, and his descendants – Amalek – are considered the worst of all enemies. In fact, it is a Mitzvah to eradicate them when identified! The fact that Hashem would save 400 of these evil monsters – and deny Dovid the opportunity to perform the Mitzvah of eradicating evil from the world – proves Hashem measures and rewards every action with precision.

**Lesson:** If Hashem rewards evil people when they are doing something positive – even with ulterior motives – imagine how much more reward Hashem will give to those who are following the Torah and doing so with pure intentions!

# V. 2018

**Question:** In 32:5, Yaakov instructs his servants that when they go to speak with Eisav ahead of him, they should address Eisav as "my lord" as a sign of respect (see notes 11 and 12 to Artscroll Ramban on this posuk). Why would Yaakov refer to Eisav with a level of respect by calling him "lord/master?"

**Answer:** The Ramban explains that it is the custom for the younger brother to show respect and honor to an older brother as if they are his father. Even though Yaakov took away Eisav's first-born rights through the sale in exchange for lentil soup, Yaakov was showing Eisav that it was as if the sale meant nothing to him – rendering it null and void – and therefore Yaakov wanted to show respect to Eisav in order to remove the hatred from his heart.

**Observation #1:** The sale of the birthright was a legitimate sale that Eisav happily agreed to! It is remarkable that Yaakov would nullify the validity of that sale – and forgo future Brachos from his father along with his burial spot in Maaras HaMachpela – just for the sake of getting Eisav to stop hating him!

**Observation #2:** Yaakov did this strategic move of calling him "lord/master" even BEFORE he encountered Eisav, at which point he then davened, sent presents, and prepared for war. This option to call him "master" wasn't a last resort – it was the FIRST option!

**Lesson:** When in a fight with people, even when we are correct, we see that by showing people respect and making them feel important (even when they are not) is a mechanism for diffusing the hatred.

# Parshas Vayeishev

## I. 2013 (Song)

*(tune of "The Ants go Marching Down")*

Vayeishev starts with Yaakov loving Yosef – his son,
More than the other children – more than the other ones,
Yosef had 2 dreams faithfully, but this created jealousy,
The brothers threw him in a pit – it was an atrocity.

Yosef was sold to Yishmaelim – who took him on a trip,
From there he went to work for Potifar, in Egypt.
Potifar's wife tried to sin, but Yosef was the one who would win,
Yosef went to jail, but soon he would prevail.

The baker and wine man had dreams – of their own,
Yosef told them what they meant – so it would be known.
The lesson we learn from Yosef, is be respectful and embrace,
Don't make others jealous, it will be a big mistake.

## II. 2014

**Background:** Yosef told his brothers of his dreams of being a monarch and ruling over them, exacerbating tensions and jealousy and precipitating his eventual sale as a slave to Egypt. This was the beginning of his downfall. Later, when Yosef is in prison in Egypt, his fellow prisoners, Pharaoh's butler and baker, both tell him their dreams. By accurately interpreting their dreams, he is eventually remembered by the butler, who informs Pharaoh, leading to Yosef's rise to power in Egypt.

**Question:** What is the difference between the two dreams that yielded different results?

**Answer:** A great Chassidic thinker once noted that Yosef's downfall began by telling others his own dreams, and his salvation began by listening to the dreams of others. He deduces from this that we are much better served listening to others and their aspirations, than by telling other people our own dreams and aspirations.

**Lesson:** Listen when other people talk and pay attention to their needs!

**Source:** http://www.partnersintorah.org/parsha-partner/vayeishev/vayeishev-5773

## III. 2015

**Question:** Yosef's brothers wanted to sentence Yosef to the death penalty. Reuven convinced them to lower him into a pit instead. His plan was to return to the pit, take Yosef out, and return him to their father Yaakov. His plan ultimately failed, as the brothers drew Yosef up out of the pit and sold him to a band of Ishmaelites. If Reuven's plan failed, why does the Torah tell us about it? Nothing tangible resulted from it!

**Answer:** Rav Boruch Halevi Epstein (who is known to us as the Torah Temima) writes that even though Reuven's plan failed, the Torah still mentions it because it is fitting to give credit to someone who does a Mitzvah.

**Lesson #1:** We get credit for a Mitzvah if we do our part, even if it doesn't come to fruition!

**Lesson #2:** We should model ourselves after the Torah, and just as the Torah talks about the positive intentions/efforts of Reuven, we should talk about the positive intentions/efforts of other people!

*Level 3 and Beyond!*

When we see someone else doing something positive, talk about it and focus on the good!

**Source:** http://ohr.edu/youth/kinder/5759/bereishi/vayeshev.htm

## IV. 2016

**Background:** The 11 brothers made a plan to kill Yosef, and this was based on the halacha that if someone is coming to hurt you, then you have to defend yourself. Reuven was the only brother who said to throw him in the pit and not kill him (and Reuven secretly wanted to come back later and save Yosef).

**Question:** Why did Reuven want to save Yosef if they already determined it was halachically acceptable proper to kill him?

**Answer:** If Reuven had let Yosef be killed, then it's possible that he would be blamed later since he was the oldest and would have been held responsible.

**Lesson:** You should always be responsible, as the oldest child, for younger children. Additionally, everyone should feel a sense of responsibility if you see other people doing the wrong thing.

**Source:** The Midrash Says, page 353

## V. 2016

**Background:** On Pharaoh's birthday, two very significant events happened. First, the butler was taken out of jail and saved. Second, the baker was killed for his crime.

**Question:** Is there a special lesson the Torah is trying to teach us about these events happening on Pharaoh's birthday?

**Our Possible Answer:** Chazal tell us that a person has special power on his birthday. In fact, some people even go to ask others for a Bracha on their birthdays. Perhaps the Torah is teaching us this very lesson regarding the very first person to ever have a birthday party in the Torah. On his very birthday, Pharaoh saved one life and took another. He raised one person up and put another down.

**Lesson:** We too have that similar power on our birthdays. We can raise people up or put others down.

## VI. 2017

**Background:** Rashi explains that Yosef was separated from Yaakov for 22 years. This was Yaakov's punishment for the 22 years that he was away from his parents and unable to fulfill the Mitzvah of Kibud Av Va'eim. (Yaakov had spent 20 years in Lavan's home and 2 years traveling back to Canaan; see Rashi to 37:34.)

**Question #1:** Yaakov was **sent** to Lavan's house by his own mother, Rivkah, when she was afraid that Eisav was going to hurt him. Why should Yaakov be punished for not being able to fulfill the Mitzvah of Kibud Av Va'eim when he was following his mother's direct orders?

**Question #2:** Even if he was held accountable for the 20 years in Lavan's house, why should he be held accountable for the 2 years of traveling? He was on his way back to do the Mitzvah?

**Our Suggested Answer:** Apparently, the Mitzvah of honoring parents is so important, that just missing out on the opportunity to do it is cause for punishment. This would be consistent with the notion that one of the few Mitzvos in the Torah that can lengthen your life is this Mitzvah of honoring parents. The Mitzvah is so important that even though Yaakov originally traveled to Lavan's

*Level 3 and Beyond!*

house following his mother's instructions, the fact that he was away for all those years and unable to fulfill that Mitzvah was a reason for his punishment!

**Lesson:** Honoring parents is a critical Mitzvah that everyone should constantly look for opportunities to perform!

# Parshas Mikeitz

## I. 2013 (Song)

*(tune of "Adon Olam")*

Mikeitz is a Parsha, where Pharaoh dreams,
About cows and grain – but he doesn't know what it means,
The butler remembers Yosef was smart,
After 7 years, the famine would start.

Pharaoh made Yosef second in command,
Only Egypt had food, so the brothers came to demand,
Food for their families, is what they asked for,
Yosef had a plan for a whole lot more.

A silver cup was hidden in Binyamin's bag,
It looked like he stole and would now have to lag,
The lesson that we learn from Yosef's plan,
Do your Hishtadlus and be a G-d fearing man.

## II. 2015

**Question:** How could Pharaoh trust Yosef, an "ex-con" who was previously a slave, to be his viceroy?

**Answer:** Rabbi Chaim Shmuelevitz teaches that when Yosef attributed his interpretations entirely to Hashem, it underscored his total honesty and trustworthiness. Pharaoh saw this Middah and realized Yosef was the person he wanted as second in command.

**Lesson:** We see how important it is to attribute everything to Hashem and be honest in everything we do!

*Level 3 and Beyond!*

**Source:** Rabbi Chaim Shmuelevitz as cited by http://www.anshe.org/parsha/miketz.htm

## III. 2016

**Background:** Menashe hid the golden goblet in Binyamin's backpack. He then went to check Reuven's and Shimon's backpack first, and eventually went to Binyamin's backpack. When Menashe took it out, all the brothers said, "You are a thief, just like your mother Rochel (referring to when Rochel stole her father's idols)."

**Question:** When the brothers accused Binyamin of being a thief, how did Binyamin respond?

**Answer:** He said nothing at all. It was only later, in private, that Binyamin told the brothers that he did not take. As a reward for Binyamin not responding when he was insulted in public, Hashem gave him the piece of land that the Beis Hamikdash will reside upon!

**Lesson:** When someone insults you, say nothing!

**Source:** Aleinu L'Shabeach, page 527 and Rabbi Juravel's Parsha Sefer, page 354

## IV. 2017

**Background:** Rashi (43:33) explains that when Yosef sat down to a meal with the brothers, Yosef seated the brothers according to their mothers and then according to their ages. For example, first he seated Leah's children, with Reuven first and Zevulun last. Then he seated Bilhah's children with Dan first, and then Zilpah's children, with Gad first. Yosef was able to seat each brother without revealing that he knew their identity because he tapped on his goblet to make it appear as if the goblet's powers were telling Yosef the order in which the brothers should be seated. Rashi explains that Binyamin was seated next to Yosef because Yosef felt, "he (Binyamin) has no mother and I have no mother, so he should sit next to me."

**Question:** It seems interesting that Yosef's reasoning for Binyamin sitting next to him was that they both did not have a living mother. Wouldn't the more logical rationale be that they were both born from the same mother? Further, that would be consistent with the logic Yosef had in assigning seats to the other brothers. He seated them all grouped by common mother. Why wouldn't he have the same logic when it came to Binyamin?

**Our Suggested Answer:** We see from Yosef's rationale that the most important thought in his mind was the sensitivity and emotional feelings of Binyamin – that they both lost a mother and that Yosef could empathize with him. This was a deeper reflection on who Yosef was and how he was conditioned to think. His priority was the sensitivity and empathy of Binyamin.

**Lesson:** We should all constantly train our minds to think like Yosef and always be emotionally sensitive to the people around us.

*Level 3 and Beyond!*

# Parshas Vayigash

## I. 2013 (Song)

*(Tune of "B-I-N-G-O")*

Vayigash starts with Yehuda pleading,
For Binyamin's well-being,

Take me instead of him,
Otherwise, we'll all be grim,
Yosef sent the servants out of the room,
"I am Yosef" in this costume.

Yosef said it's Hashgacha Pratis,
Hashem planned all this,

Go back home today,
Get my Daddy this way,
Tell him to bring the whole family,
The number of people was 70.

Yaakov sent Yehuda in motion,
To learn Torah in Goshen,

Yosef saw Yaakov and cheered,
They hugged and shed some tears,
The lesson from Yosef's revelation,
Don't embarrass and cause frustration.

## II. 2015 (Part 1)

**Question:** How did Yosef try to make his brother's feel better after he revealed himself and they were embarrassed?

*Level 3 and Beyond!*

**Answer:** He said it was all part of Hashem's plan and that Hashem did all this so that he could feed their family during the famine.

**Lesson:** Be sensitive and look for ways to eliminate the embarrassment of others!

## III. 2015 (Part 2)

**Question:** What did Yosef tell the brothers before they left?

**Answer:** Two things: Don't fight about blaming each other and don't fight about Torah either because it could distract them from the dangers on the road.

**Lesson #1:** Stay focused on your objective!
**Lesson #2:** Don't fight!

## IV. 2016

**Background:** Yosef and Binyamin cried on each other's necks (45:14). The Midrash says that they each had a Nevuah (prophesy). Binyamin was crying because he saw in the future, Yosef's land of Shiloh would have the Mishkan destroyed. Yosef was crying because he saw in the future, Binyamin's land would have both Batei Mikdash destroyed. They were crying for each other.

**Question:** Why did they cry about each other's problems instead of their own?

**Answer:** Rabbi Yechezkel Kuzmir explains that when we hear about someone else's pain, we should feel it the same way. That's exactly what Yosef and Binyamin did.

*Level 3 and Beyond!*

**Lesson:** We should always look to empathize with the pain of others, even when we have our own troubles.

**Source:** Rabbi Yechezkel Kuzmir as cited by Torahfax email on January 2, 2017

# V. 2017

**Background:** Chazal explain that when Yosef went to greet his father after years of being apart, Yosef fell on his father's neck, but Yaakov did not reciprocate and did not even kiss Yosef, as Yaakov was busy saying the Shema and could not interrupt it.

**Question:** Why did Yaakov decide to say Shema at this exact moment? And if this was the time to say it, why wasn't Yosef saying it as well? What was so special about the reunion that caused Yaakov to say Shema at that moment?

**Answer:** The Zera Shimshon explains that the words "Shema" and "Echad" – both of which have enlarged letters ("ayin" and "daled") – contain a hidden meaning. The "daled" is the Gematria (numerical value) of 4, which alludes to the four matriarchs (e.g., Sarah, Rivkah, Rochel, and Leah). The "ayin" is the Gematria of 70, which alludes to unique contributions from each of the Avos: Avraham built 70 bridges of Chesed, Yitzchak (representing strict judgement) was responsible for the 70 elders of the Sanhedrin, and Yaakov was the father (or grandfather) of 70 people who entered Egypt. Each one of the Avos had a unique contribution that related to the number 70. Therefore, the "ayin" was representative of the Avos/Patriarchs and the "daled" was representative of the Imos/Matriarchs. When Yaakov was greeted by Yosef, it was the first time that all 70 souls were together – and therefore his contribution of the "70 souls coming to Egypt" was suddenly complete. With this excitement in mind, knowing that the Shema would now be whole, he recited it immediately, knowing it was at that moment that triggered its completion.

Further, when you remove the large letters "ayin" and "daled," the remaining letters from those two words can be rearranged to spell "Esmach – I will be happy." Yaakov was showing how happy he was to see his entire family reunited for the first time and that the Shema could now be said properly!

**Lesson:** When Yaakov realized his contribution was completed, he immediately acted on his inspiration and recited the Shema. When we experience moments of inspiration or happiness, we should act on it immediately and thank Hashem, showing how much we appreciate and recognize His involvement.

**Source:** Zera Shimshon, Artscroll Volume 1, page 171-172

*Level 3 and Beyond!*

# Parshas Vayechi

## I. 2013 (Song)

*(tune of "Wheels on the Bus Go Round and Round")*

Vayechi's the last Parsha in Bereishis,
All the brothers have now made peace,
Yosef asked his daddy Yaakov,
Give Brachos to Menashe and Ephraim in droves.

Each of the tribes got a special Bracha,
They loved it and were struck with awe,
Yaakov then went to live with Hashem,
In Maras HaMachpela.

Yosef knew his time was near,
He said there was nothing to fear,
But he wanted to be buried in Israel,
He knew this was ideal.

The lesson we learn from the tribes,
With the Brachos that describe,
Everybody has something special to them,
And it comes from Hashem.

## II. 2015

**Question:** According to Rashi (48:16), Yaakov blessed Ephraim and Menashe that they should be like fish, noting that fish are fruitful and are not affected by the evil eye. Why did Yaakov choose to bless them like fish, out of the thousands of living creatures?

**Answer:** The commentators explain that Kosher fish are unique among Kosher animals in that once a fish possesses the requisite Kosher signs, there is nothing that can make the fish non-Kosher. On the other hand, even if Kosher animals possess the requisite traits, they can become non-Kosher if they are improperly slaughtered, die without slaughter, or possess a critical defect such as a hole in the lung. Therefore Yaakov blessed Ephraim and Menashe that they should be like fish, in the sense that they should never lose their pure status. How fitting it is that this is the blessing with which Jewish fathers bless their children on Friday nights and other special occasions.

**Lesson:** When we give Brachos to the children on Friday night, we should remember that we are giving them the Bracha that they should never lose their status of being pure.

**Source:** http://www.partnersintorah.org/parsha-partner/vayechi-5770

## III. 2016 (Part 1)

**Question:** Why did Yaakov single out Ephraim and Menashe as the prototypes whom everyone would wish to emulate? Why do we give our children the Bracha on Friday night to be like Menashe and Ephraim? Why not any of the other brothers?

**Answer #1:** Menashe and Ephraim were the only ones who grew up in Egypt, surrounded by a non-Jewish society. Yet they kept the Torah as learned from Yosef. We want our children to keep the Torah no matter what environment they are in!

**Answer #2:** When Yaakov switched his hands around, Yosef objected, but Menashe remained silent and was not jealous as all!

Upon seeing Menashe's reaction, Yaakov said: "let these two brothers be the examples for all Israel to follow."

**Lesson:** This is one of the reasons we give the Bracha to our children on Friday night: that they should emulate the traits of Menashe and Ephraim and (a) keep the Torah even when they are in a society where most people don't and (b) not be jealous of other people. Be happy for them!

**Sources:** Living Each Week (Rabbi Avraham Twerski) and http://www.anshe.org/parsha/vayechi.htm and Artscroll Siddur commentary by Friday night Brachos.

# IV. 2016 (Part 2)

**Statement #1:** The Gemara says that Yaakov called all his sons around him and wanted to reveal when Mashiach was coming. Hashem didn't want this to happen (because otherwise people wouldn't behave properly in the meantime and would not anticipate Mashiach in the same way). Yaakov thought that perhaps one of his sons wasn't worthy and that's why Ruach Hakodesh left him. In response to this, the brothers all said, "Shema Yisroel Hashem Elokeinu Hashem Echad." Meaning to say, "We all believe what you believe." Yaakov was relieved that they were all accepting of his statement and responded, "Baruch Shem Kevod..."

**Statement #2:** The Targum Yonason says that alternatively, Yaakov responded, "Yehei Shemei Rabbah Mevorach...." instead of, "Baruch Shem Kevod..."

**Question:** So which was it: "Baruch Shem Kevod..." or "Yehei Shemei Rabbah...?"

**Answer:** In reality, they both mean the same thing, except one is in Hebrew (Baruch Shem Kevod) and one is in Aramaic (Yehei Shemei

Rabbah). In essence, they both mean that Hashem's name should be blessed forever and that the whole world should recognize this! So it's the same thing!

**Lesson:** Let us remember the importance of saying "Baruch Shem Kevod…" and "Yehei Shemei Rabbah…," and that in essence, they both mean that Hashem's name should be blessed forever and the whole world should recognize this.

**Source:** See the Feldheim Sefer "Just One Word: Amen," pages 104-105

# V. 2017 (Part 1)

**Background:** Yaakov asked Yosef to bury him in Canaan. Yosef swore that he would and Yaakov thanked him. The Baal HaTurim (47:31) says that the word V'yishtachavu (which means Yaakov thanked Yosef) equals 730, which is equal to the Hebrew phrase "Modim Al B'Sorah Tova – Thanks should be given upon hearing good news." [We note that it equals 729, but in Gematria (numerical value), being off by one still counts as being equal. This is for a variety of reasons, which are beyond the scope of this write-up.]

**Question:** Why is it considered such good news that Yosef agreed to bury Yaakov in Canaan? Wasn't it expected that Yosef would want to do his father's last wish?

**Our Suggested Answer:** Perhaps we see that you should never take for granted when somebody does you a favor. Yaakov was expressing his appreciation to Yosef in an excited way – that it was good news – and not making an assumption that it was simply "coming to him."

*Level 3 and Beyond!* 57

**Lesson:** You should always express appreciation when someone does you a favor and consider it to be good news, even if you expect it. Never take anything for granted!

## VI. 2017 (Part 2)

**Background:** Towards the end of Yaakov's life, as he was giving instructions for where to be buried, the posuk tells us (47:31) that Yaakov bowed his head towards the end of his bed. In Rashi's second explanation, Rashi explains that Yaakov prostrated himself to Hashem because his children were perfect and not one of them was wicked. Rashi continues and says this is evidenced by the fact that Yosef was a king, and furthermore, even though he was captured among the non-Jews, he remained steadfast in his righteousness. [Rashi quoting from Sifrei Va'eschanan 31, Sifrei Haazinu 334].

**Question:** How could Yaakov say that all his children were perfect? It is understandable that none of them were wicked. But how could Yaakov declare them perfect, when there were several instances highlighting their flaws over the course of Sefer Bereishis, such as:

- Reuven moved his father's bed from Bilhah's tent to Leah's tent after Rochel died. This was done without permission and as a sign of disrespect. In fact, prior to this incident, Reuven was supposed to receive the Kehunah and be a Kohein, but after he made this error, he was no longer eligible to receive the Kehunah.
- When Shimon and Levi exacted revenge on the city of Shechem for what they did to Dina, Yaakov rebuked them for using excessive force.
- When the brothers threw Yosef into the pit, although the brothers felt fully justified, the Torah reveals to us that their judgment also had a slight trace of jealousy. Since the brothers' deed was tainted by jealousy, both they and future generations had to suffer the consequences. Rabbeinu Yonah says that the Sinas Chinam (baseless hatred) for which the

second Beis Hamikdash was destroyed was an echo of the hatred of Yosef's brothers. (See Rabbi Leff's Sefer on Outlooks and Insights on this point; see here also: http://www.aish.com/tp/i/oai/Yosef-and-His-Brothers-The-Anatomy-of-a-Sale.htm)

**Given these examples above, how could Yaakov call them perfect?**

**Rochel's Suggested Answer:** Yaakov was teaching us that a parent will always look at their children in a positive way, even if they make mistakes! Additionally, perhaps Yaakov was upset at each of them at the time of their actions, but as time went on, Yaakov looked at each of the tribes in a special way!

**Another Suggested Answer:** Despite making mistakes, a person can still be considered perfect if they repent and do teshuva. In all areas where the 12 tribes made errors, and even in the cases where they were punished for their flaws – they eventually did teshuva and repented. Their focus was always to grow and become connected to Hashem. Yaakov is telling us that even if you make a mistake – and get punished for it – as long as you perform a completed teshuva for your actions and remain constantly attached to Hashem, you may still be considered perfect!

**Lesson:** We should learn from our mistakes and commit to improving. Doing so may be more than just good motivation – Hashem might consider it as if we returned to a state of perfection!

# VII. 2018

**Question:** When Yaakov gave Brachos to each of his children, the only ones who he calls "brothers" are Shimon and Levi. Why didn't Yaakov call any of his other children "brothers?"

**Answer:** The Ramban explains (49:5) that Shimon and Levi had the character trait of brotherhood more than anyone else because of how they went to destroy the city of Shechem because of the incident with Dina. Although what they did was wrong, Yaakov was defending Shimon and Levi, asking Hashem to lessen their punishment because they did it with good intentions – all for their sister. Yaakov was saying that they were the ultimate "brothers" – ones who cared about their sister – and therefore should not be punished so harshly.

**Observation:** One may have thought that the "family member argument" would have been more of a reason for Shimon/Levi to be biased and therefore due to the full extent of the punishment! Yet, we see from this Ramban that protecting your family members has only a positive connotation to it!

**Lesson:** Care for your brothers, sisters, and family members!

# Parshas Shemos

## I. 2013 (Song)

*(tune of "Pop Goes the Weasel")*

Shemos starts with Jews being enslaved, by bad King Pharaoh,
He said "Throw all baby boys, into the Nile."
Shifra and Puah were midwives, who didn't hurt the babies,
Yocheved had baby Moshe and protected him like a good lady.

Basya found baby Moshe, floating in the river,
He grew up in Pharaoh's palace, the Jews he would deliver.
Moshe saw people hurting one other, he said "This is not OK,"
He went to live with Yisro, and married Tziporah one day.

Moshe was watching Yisro's sheep, he saw a bush on fire,
It was Hashem speaking to him, telling him to aspire.
Moshe and Aaron went to Pharaoh, said "Let my people go,"
The lesson we learn from Moshe is you always have to grow.

*[Explanation of Lesson: Moshe thought he was inferior when talking to Hashem, and Hashem insisted, knowing Moshe's potential and what he could accomplish. We have to recognize how much we can accomplish, as long as we are willing to learn and grow.]*

## II. 2015

**Question:** When Moshe took care of Yisro's sheep, he would take them far away from their home into open fields. Most shepherds would keep the sheep as close to home as possible. Why did Moshe take them out into the middle of nowhere?

*Level 3 and Beyond!*

**Answer:** Moshe was concerned that the sheep would eat the grass on someone else's property and he wanted to be careful that the sheep would not steal from anyone else's property. That's why he took them as far away into the open fields as possible!

**Lesson:** Be careful with others' property!

**Source:** Little Midrash Says, page 22

# III. 2016

**Question:** The Midrash Rabbah (Vayikra 1:3) mentions that Moses actually had ten names. Nonetheless, Hashem decided to call Moshe, the name that Basya (Pharaoh's daughter) called him. Why did Hashem choose this name of Moshe above all the other names? [Even stranger, the reason why Basya called him "Moshe" was because it corresponds to her act of pulling him out of the water. If so, it does not describe Moses at all; rather it describes the conduct of Basya!] So why did Hashem choose to call him by that name?

**Answer:** Rabbi Chaim Shmuelevitz explains that when Basya defied the decree of her father, Pharaoh, and saved Moshe from the Nile, she exhibited a high level of self-sacrifice for the benefit of an unknown child. This altruistic act of Chesed to help a baby that she didn't even know, penetrated into the very being of the infant Moshe. It was mirrored in Moshe throughout his life.

**Lesson:** We have to feel the suffering of other people and help them in the best way we can. This will make us true leaders!

**Source:** Rabbi Chaim Shmuelevitz cited in www.shemayisrael.com/parsha/kahn/archives/vayikra69.htm

# IV. 2017

**Background:** The Baal HaTurim explains (2:5) Basya went down to the river to convert to being Jewish. Once there, she heard Aharon crying out of fear that something would happen to his baby brother. According to the Paaneach Raza (on the Baal HaTurim 2:6), the reason Basya took Moshe out of the river is that Aharon was crying.

**Question:** Why did Aharon's crying cause Basya to take Moshe out of the river? Why wasn't it that Basya wanted to take him out for the Chesed of helping a baby? Or, it could have been that Basya knew he was Jewish and was special (and she herself was converting to Judaism!). What was it about Aharon's crying that triggered her actions?

**Answer:** We see the power of crying and what it can cause another person to do. It is implied from the Paaneach Raza that had Aharon not been crying, Basya would have left Moshe in the river and not taken him out! Crying has the power to elicit strong emotions from other people. When you see another person crying, you should immediately help them, as it means they are going through an emotionally difficult time.

**Lesson:** When you see other people crying, help them and empathize with their pain.

**Source:** Paaneach Raza (on the Baal HaTurim 2:6). Paaneach Raza was Rav Yitzchak ben Yehuda HaLevi of France, 13th Century, printed in Prague in 1607.

# V. 2018

**Background:** Rashi (2:3) notes that when Moshe was placed in the basket down the river as an infant, there was only tar on the outside of the basket, but not on the inside. The reason for this, says Rashi, is because Hashem didn't want there to be the foul odor of tar in the presence of the little Tzadik.

## PART 1

**Question #1:** Moshe had not yet performed any acts of greatness. Why was Hashem rewarding/protecting him with an odor-free experience when he did not yet rise to the level of a Tzadik?

**Question #2:** Moshe was just a baby and was not in the basket for a long period of time. What damage could possibly be inflicted from an extremely temporary odor? Moshe would never remember the experience!

**Our Suggested Answer:** Hashem's calculations are exact and He knows what we can handle and what we need. Despite Moshe not yet proving his great capabilities, it being a temporary situation, and him being just an infant, Hashem ensured Moshe would have an environment commensurate with who he destined to be.

**Lesson:** Similar to Moshe, we are sometimes "placed in a basket" into situations that we cannot control, nor did we ask for. No matter what stage of your life mission you are on – even if you did not exhibit your great potential at that moment – Hashem will create circumstances and surroundings that are meant specifically for you!

## PART 2

**Question:** We know that Noach's ark was filled with tar on the inside and the outside and yet, Noach was called a Tzadik by the

Torah as well. Why was one Tzadik (Moshe) spared the bad smell of tar on the inside while another Tzadik (Noach) wasn't?

**Our Suggested Answer:** Rabbi Monsour quotes the Arizal, who teaches us that Moshe was a Gilgul (reincarnation) of Noach's soul, which returned to this world to correct this grave mistake which it had made. The flood is blamed on Noach because when he heard about the impending catastrophe, he did not pray to Hashem for mercy or try to inspire the people of his time to change. He instead simply complied with Hashem's instructions to build an ark to save himself, his family and the animals. He rescued himself without trying to rescue the people. This is in contrast to Moshe, who said to Hashem, after the sin of the Golden Calf, not to eradicate the Jewish People and pleaded on their behalf, saying to remove his name from the Torah instead. By sacrificing his own future for the sake of the Jewish people, refusing to be rescued as the people are destroyed, Moshe rectified the mistake of Noah. (see http://www.dailyhalacha.com/m/parasha.aspx?id=531)

Based on this explanation provided by the Arizal as quoted by Rabbi Mansour, perhaps we can suggest that the difference between the Tzadik of Noach and the Tzadik of Moshe was the ability to be connected to others during the time of trouble. As Moshe was concerned for the welfare of others, Hashem decreed that therefore the small ark carrying him would be odor free!

**Lesson:** When you make other people the priority and care about them, Hashem makes you the priority and takes care of you, Middah Keneged Middah!

# VI. 2019

**Question:** The posuk says, "The child grew up...it happened in those days that Moshe grew up and went out to his brethren and observed their burdens; and he saw an Egyptian man striking a Hebrew man, of his brethren" (Shemos 2:10-11). Why does the Torah repeat that Moshe grew up twice?

**Answer:** The Ramban (2:10) explains that the first phrase refers to Moshe's attainment of physical maturity. The second phrase refers to Moshe's growth in intellectual and spiritual maturity, becoming "a man of understanding." The Torah then specifies the sign of Moshe's spiritual maturity was the fact that he went out to his brothers and saw their labors. Rashi comments on this phrase that Moshe contemplated their plight and "applied his eyes and heart to suffer with them."

**Our Observation:** There were many other aspects of Moshe's life that one could have pointed to as a spiritual "growing up" moment. Incidents such as interacting with Hashem at the burning bush for the first time, agreeing to lead the Jewish people despite his speech impediment, the respect he showed for the evil Pharaoh, and executing the miracles of the ten plagues are just a few that stand out. Yet, the Torah tells us that the pivotal moment that Moshe "grew up" spiritually is when he went out and saw the pain of his fellow Jews. The sign of a truly great person is one who feels the empathy and pain of other Jews who are suffering.

**Lesson:** When you hear about another person going through a tough situation, be sensitive, daven for them, and feel their pain as if it were your own!

# Parshas Vaeira

## I. 2013 (Song)

*(tune of "Imagination – the Figment Ride Song in Epcot Center")*

Vaeira starts with Moshe and Aaron,
Coming to Pharaoh, saying "Let My People Go,"
Aaron made a stick, turn to a snake,
Pharaoh's magicians said "We too can make."

Imagination was their interpretation,
No Inspiration, only frustration.

7 plagues are in this Parsha,
Blood, frogs, and lice were the first ones they saw,
Then came the wild beasts, pestilence, and boils,
Hail didn't stop Jews from their toil.

Plagues didn't impress the mighty Pharaoh,
He still would not let them go.
The lesson of the seven Makos,
Listen to Hashem, and don't oppose.

## II. 2015

**Question:** Aharon brought about the plagues of blood, frogs, and lice. Why not Moshe?

**Answer:** In order to bring about these plagues, Aharon had to hit the river (which brought about the plagues of blood and frogs) and the sand (which brought about the plague of lice). Since the river saved Moshe when he was a baby and the sand saved Moshe when he

*Level 3 and Beyond!*

buried the Egyptian under it, Hashem didn't want Moshe hitting these creations, as it would be a lack of Hakaras HaTov.

**Lesson:** If Moshe was thankful to the river and sand, all the more so we have to be thankful to the many people in our lives!

**Source:** Little Midrash Says, page 50

# III. 2016 (Part 1)

**Background:** Aharon brought about the plagues of blood, frogs, and lice due to the Hakaras HaTov that Moshe had to the river and the sand.

**Question:** Does it make a difference to the water of the Nile or to the dirt of Egypt, objects which cannot feel and cannot think, whether they are stricken by Aharon instead of by Moshe? How is it possible for inanimate objects to feel a sense of Hakaras HaTov expressed by a grateful human being?

**Answer:** Rabbi Frand explains that we learn from this that the exercise of expressing gratitude is not for the benefit of the person who gave the favor, but for the benefit of the person who received the favor. When a person is a recipient of any type of gift or favor, it creates an obligation on him to show his appreciation. Whether the "benefactor" of the favor can appreciate the gratitude being demonstrated or not is, in fact, secondary.

**Lesson:** A person must go through life realizing that people and things provide favors for him on many different occasions. The person is obligated to express that Hakaras HaTov because such expression transforms him as a person.

# IV. 2016 (Part 2)

**Question:** During the plague of the wild animals, where did the animals come from and what did they bring with them?

**Answer:** They came from all over the world and brought their weather with them. For example, when the polar bear came, he brought the freezing cold weather and anytime an Egyptian would come near the polar bear, the Egyptian would have to wear a coat. Then, when an elephant came and got close to an Egyptian, the person would be very hot and have to take off the coat! This made life miserable for the Egyptians. [Rabbi Juravel, page 81].

**Our Observation:** Perhaps a deeper meaning to this is that we have to be careful who we associate with and get "close to." When we are around "cold" people, we absorb some of their negative energy and "need a coat." Alternatively, when we are around "warm" people, we likewise become good-natured like them.

**Lesson:** Look for people who are positive influences and get close to them!

# V. 2016 (Part 3)

**Question:** Rashi comments that in some places Aharon is mentioned before Moshe and in other places, the order is reversed. This is to teach us that they were equal. Yet, since Moshe was the greatest prophet and sage of all time, to such an extent that Hashem chose to give the Torah through Moshe, how can it be said that Aharon, for all his merits, was Moshe's "equal?"

**Answer #1:** Although Moshe's power was greater than Aharon's, they were still considered equals since they were both needed for the redemption of the Jews. By analogy, even though one business partner may have a greater role than the other, if the business cannot function without both of them, they are equals in that sense.

**Answer #2:** Like Moshe, Aharon performed Hashem's will throughout his life to the utmost of his ability and with complete faith. Both Moshe and Aharon devoted themselves completely and wholeheartedly to the things which they were given to do. Moshe and Aharon, even though they differed in their abilities, could be considered equals since they both achieved their full potential. In Hashem's eyes, success is measured by how well we fulfill our personal mission.

**Lesson:** Fulfill the potential you were given!

**Source:** Rav Moshe Feinstein in his Sefer Darash Moshe

# VI. 2017

**Background:** The Baal HaTurim (6:2) says that the word "Vaeira" has the same Gematria (numerical value) as the word "Yitzchak" to teach you that Yitzchak caused the Jews to leave Egypt at the time that they did (after 210 years of slavery instead of the original decree of 400 years).

**Question:** What did Yitzchak do to merit the Jews' early departure from Egypt?

**Answer:** For the entire time that the Jews were enslaved, the three Avos (Avraham, Yitzchak, and Yaakov) cried before Hashem, asking Him to let the Jewish people go. Hashem said, "Is there anyone who is willing to change the letters in their name to reduce the years of slavery by the Gematria of those letters?" Avraham and Yaakov both said no, but Yitzchak said he would change the letter Tzadi in his name to a Shin. The difference between the Shin (300) and the Tzadi (90) is 210, which is the exact number of years that the Jews were in

Egypt and were then freed! By Yitzchak being Mevater (e.g., giving up one of the letters in his name), he allowed the Jews to come out of Egypt much sooner than Hashem had originally planned!

**Lesson:** This is the power of being Mevater (giving in)!

**Source:** Peirush Harosh, as quoted in the Baal HaTurim to 6:2 (see Artscroll Baal HaTurim, page 571, footnote #8)

# VII. 2018

**Background:** During the plague of frogs, the posuk refers to the "frog" in the singular. Rashi (8:2) says this could be one of two possibilities. Either (a) there was one giant frog who came out of the Nile and as the Egyptians hit it, the frog multiplied into many others or (b) the swarming of the frogs is referred to as singular ("Lashon Yechidus"), as they were all like one.

**Question:** We know that the frogs went everywhere and did different things: some jumped into the ovens and died, others jumped into people's food, yet other frogs were just jumping around and croaking, creating general havoc for the Egyptians. This being the case, how could Rashi say in his second explanation that they were all considered like one, where the frogs all had separate roles?

**Our Suggested Answer:** Even when people have different jobs and roles, if they have the same goal, they are unified by that mission. The frogs were tasked with disrupting the lives of the Egyptians and they were willing to do anything to achieve that goal – whether it was jumping in their beds, bothering the Egyptians through croaking, or killing themselves by jumping into the ovens. But their mission of carrying out Hashem's wish was one and the same, and therefore they were considered as "Lashon Yechidus," as if they were like one.

**Lesson:** Every person has unique talents and different skills. But as long as we all have the same goal – to live a Torah lifestyle and connect to Hashem – we are all unified and connected as one people!

# VIII. 2019

**Background:** The Torah says (6:9) that the Jewish people didn't listen to Moshe because of "shortness of spirit and hard work." The Ramban on this posuk clarifies that while the Jewish people believed in Hashem and that Moshe was His messenger, they didn't pay attention to Moshe because of the "shortness of spirit and hard work."

**Question:** What is the difference between "shortness of spirit" and "hard work?"

**Answer:** The Ramban explains:
- "Shortness of spirit" – the fear that Pharaoh will kill them
- "Hard work" – the pressure of the taskmasters was so intense that they didn't have a minute to hear or reflect on anything other than work. Essentially, they were kept so busy that they didn't "have a minute to think."

Both of these combined together caused the Jews to have the mentality that even though they knew intellectually that their suffering would eventually end, it was not enough to make them feel any better since the pain was unbearable at that time. The Ramban compares this to a person who is undergoing such a bad illness that even if he knows it will eventually end, the pain is so unbearable that it does not give him the desire to want to continue to live.

**Our Observation:** The Jews did not have the will to live because of the combination of those two factors mentioned above. This implies that if one of those factors was eliminated, they would have regained the will to live. The second factor – hard work – involved keeping them busy all hours of the day. Had they simply taken a short amount of time to reflect on what Moshe was saying, they would have overcome the other fear that Pharaoh would kill them! That small moment in reflection would have catapulted them into conquering their fears, thereby enabling them to pay attention to what Moshe was saying. A small investment of reflection could have removed their fears and reignited their will to live.

**Lesson:** Sometimes we get so caught up in the daily grind of life that we don't take a minute to stop, reflect, or think about how Hashem is active in our lives or what the "messengers" (like Moshe!) are telling us. We have fears and sometimes very significant problems, but if we would stop and think about the Torah, Emunah, and how Hashem runs the world, it is very likely that we will overcome our fears!

# Parshas Bo

## I. 2013 (Song)

*(tune of "Shalom Aleichem")*

Parshas Bo finishes the 10 plagues, on Pharaoh and his aides,
The last 3 Makos continued to warn, they were locusts, darkness, and the firstborn.

After the 10$^{th}$ plague, Pharaoh was swayed,
He told the Jews to go away,
The Jews left quickly, took their Matzah in a jiffy,
Gold, silver, and clothing they got – it was nifty.

The very first Mitzvah, given to the Jews, was Rosh Chodesh,
We start the month brand new and fresh, and the moon we get to bless.

Celebrate this win – with Pesach, Matzah, and Tefillin,
The lesson we learn, from the Egyptians,
Mistakes are normal, as long as they're not formal
Do better next time, that will be a good sign.

## II. 2015

**Question:** Kiddush Hachodesh (the sanctification of the new moon) was the very first commandment given to the Jewish nation as a whole, which suggests that this is a most important Mitzvah. What is its significance?

**Answer:** Rosh Chodesh, the start of the new month, symbolizes renewal. Just as the moon disappears at the end of each month but returns and grows to fullness, so too the Jewish nation has the ability to rise up from oblivion and restore itself to past greatness. This essential characteristic of the Jews was first demonstrated in Egypt when the Jewish people had fallen to the 49th level of impurity, one level above spiritual extinction. They renewed themselves to such a degree that only seven weeks later they were able to stand at Mount Sinai, receive the Torah, and experience prophecy!

**Lesson:** Everyone makes mistakes. The problem is that when a person feels guilty about what he has done wrong and sees himself as a failure, he may give up and lose the strength to keep trying. In order to avoid this, one must recognize that although mistakes were made, we can always get back up and start again.

**Source:** Artscroll Chumash, Stone edition, see also http://www.aish.com/tp/b/1-min-vort/288962221.html

# III. 2016

**Question:** This week's Parsha contains the Mitzvah of Sipur Yitzias Mitzrayim (telling our children the events of the exodus from Egypt). Why do so many Mitzvos, prayers, and blessings center on this event? The Tefillin, Mezuzah, Shema, Kiddush on Shabbos, Bircas HaMazon, and countless other Mitzvos all remind us of Yitzias Mitzrayim. Why do we focus so much on this event?

**Answer:** The Sefer HaChinuch (Mitzvah 21) explains that Hashem, by taking us out of Egypt, proved to the entire world that He is in control of everything. Not only that, He changed the laws of nature for the Jewish people. This is a basic pillar in our Emunah (faith). It explains Hashem's might and how we came to be His nation. Therefore, every Pesach, fathers tell over their family history (Yitzias Mitzrayim) to their sons, explaining how Hashem changed the life of our nation in a most miraculous way.

**Mashal/Story**: There was once a king who went hunting in the forest. He met a young shepherd there and was amazed by his intelligence. The king took the shepherd back to his palace and hired tutors for him. The boy grew to become a very wise man, and the king appointed him to be in charge of his storehouses. The other officers of the king were jealous of this former shepherd, so they fabricated a story to turn the king against him. They claimed that he was stealing from the king's storehouses and using the money to beautify his own home. The king reluctantly summoned the former shepherd and told him that he must inspect his home, in order to see if the charges were substantiated. They went together to his home, and the king found it to be very simply furnished. They went from room to room and there was absolutely no evidence of embezzlement. They came to a room with a locked door. The king asked, "What is in this room?" The officer replied in a low voice, "Nothing, my king. Please let us return to the palace." The king's suspicion was aroused. He asked the officer to open the door. The officer begged the king to spare him humiliation and leave the door locked. The king insisted and the door was opened. The king entered the room and found an old shepherd's bag, walking stick and flute. Why did the officer keep these things in a locked room? The former shepherd explained that from the day that the king brought him to the palace, he never forgot that he was once a lowly shepherd. Twice each day he sat in this room to remind himself of this and to reinforce his gratitude to the king. When the king heard this, he knew that the charges against this former shepherd were false and that he was a loyal servant.

**Lesson:** Yitzias Mitzrayim is such an integral part of our daily lives because of the key principle of our faith. We need to constantly remember on a daily basis that Hashem is the one who controls the world and everything is Hashgacha Pratis!

**Source:** The Sefer "613 Stories on the Taryag Mitzvos" by M. Frankel. See also http://ohr.edu/youth/kinder/5759/shmos/bo.htm

## IV. 2017

**Question:** The Torah says that after Moshe Rabbeinu commanded the Jewish people concerning the laws of Pesach on Rosh Chodesh Nissan, "The Jewish people went and did what they were commanded" (12:28). The Mechilta asks: Did they then fulfill these commandments immediately?

**Answer:** No, they did not. The first Mitzvah didn't become practicable until the tenth of Nissan when they purchased the lamb for the Korban Pesach. But since they committed themselves to fulfill these Mitzvos, the Torah considers it as if they fulfilled them immediately.

**Lesson:** Rabbi Zev Leff explains that one who commits himself to fulfilling all the Mitzvos gets rewarded immediately even for the ones he cannot yet physically do or does not yet know. Since he is committed to fulfill whatever Mitzvos will come his way, the commitment itself is considered their fulfillment!

## V. 2018

**Background:** The firstborn of every Kosher animal is sacrificed to Hashem. However, there is only one non-Kosher animal that is redeemed – the donkey. While the donkey is not consecrated in the same way a Kosher animal is, it is still redeemed in a special way. In his second explanation, Rashi (13:13) explains that when we left Egypt, the donkeys assisted us by carrying the gold and silver. According to this explanation of Rashi, it seems that the Jews are expressing Hakaras HaTov to the donkey for all the heavy carrying they did for us and therefore we redeem its firstborn.

**Question #1:** The donkey is an animal who is used to carrying heavy loads and not taking a break (that's why Yaakov blessed Yisaschar to be like a donkey!). Its job is to carry heavy objects. Why should we give the donkey such a special status for work it's used to doing anyway?

**Question #2:** We could possibly understand a one-time reward to the donkeys for their efforts in carrying the gold and silver. But why issue all donkeys – and their descendants – a reward that lasts forever? Doesn't this seem a bit extreme?

**Question #3:** A donkey doesn't have any emotions or feelings. Is the donkey going to appreciate this Hakaras HaTov shown to them? Further, are any of its descendants really going to understand what is happening to them and why?

**Our Suggested Answer:** When it comes to expressing gratitude, the Torah is telling us that even if it's someone's job to do something – like the donkey – you still have to express gratitude. When a clerk checks you out at the supermarket, you have to express appreciation for the job they are doing even though that's what they are supposed to be doing. Further, while it is possible that sometimes a simple "thank you" is enough, there are other times that we need to go the extra mile and show how much we value the other person's help. Finally, the Torah is telling us that expressing Hakaras HaTov does more for the one issuing the "thank you" than the recipient – and that's why we do it perpetually for generations to come because it helps US remember the Chesed done for us and changes us as people.

**Lesson:** We need to express appreciation to those who are doing their jobs in a way that shows them how much we appreciate their work. Additionally, expressing Hakaras HaTov helps us even more than it helps the recipient!

# VI. 2019

**Question:** After the plague of darkness, Pharaoh told Moshe that everyone can leave and go out for the holiday of the Korban Pesach (see 10:9), but the Jews must leave their flocks and cattle behind (10:24). Why did Pharaoh want them to leave animals in Egypt?

**Answer:** The Ramban (10:24) explains that all of the Jews' wealth was concentrated in livestock (e.g., animals), so Pharaoh thought that they would come back for their wealth after their holiday was over. The Ramban continues to explain that even if they did escape, at least Pharaoh would have lots of wealth left over from them!

**Observation #1:** Didn't Pharaoh realize that if Hashem was powerful enough to do all of these miracles, wouldn't He be able to sustain the Jews and replace any wealth that they had previously lost? Yet Pharaoh believed that the Jews' desire for money would overcome any intellectual recognition of this fact.

**Observation #2:** The Jews were slaves, their babies were murdered, and they were tormented for hundreds of years. Once they were out, how could Pharaoh have possibly thought they would come back for their money and risk being enslaved all over again? Apparently, he understood the draw of money and how powerful it could be.

**Lesson:** We see how careful we have to be when it comes to money. It can blind us and make us oblivious to the realities that Hashem is in control.

*Level 3 and Beyond!*

# Parshas Beshalach

## I. 2014 (Song)

*(tune of "Under the Sea")*

Beshalach begins as the Jews leave,
Egyptians still don't believe,

Jews got to the Red Sea,
Got scared and began to plead.

Just look to the world around you,
And know Hashem is there for you.

Trust in Him with all your heart
You see even the sea can part – uh oh!

Under the sea, right through the sea,
Jews walked free, filled up with glee, naturally.

The Mitzrim drowned in tons of sea, all of them filled with misery, it was a shock, they tried to flock to find safety.

After the Neis of the sea splitting,
Jews sang a song quite fitting.

Hashem gave them water and food,
Each day the Ma'an was renewed.

Amalek came to battle the Jews,
Moshe's hands helped Amalek lose.

The lesson we learn from the Parsha,
Trust Hashem to give you Maana!

Under the sea, right through the sea,
Jews walked free, filled up with glee, naturally.

The Mitzrim drowned in tons of sea, all of them filled with misery, it was a shock, they tried to flock to find safety.

# II. 2015

**Question:** Regarding the Yam Suf, the Midrash is filled with details of the "special features" which occurred during the splitting of the sea. The Midrash describes that if a woman was holding a young child who was crying, she would stretch out her hand, and from the water she would retrieve an apple or a pomegranate to calm the child. If a child was thirsty, they could drink from the sweet, drinkable water of the sea. The paths between the walls of water were as dry as concrete. These details of Krias Yam Suf lead us to ask: Why did Hashem find it necessary to make these secondary miracles? Was it not enough that He split the sea?

**Answer:** Rav Chaim Shmulevitz answers this question with the following parable: If a person sees a woman caring for a baby, there is a sure way to know if it is the mother or a nanny. If after the woman bathes or changes the baby, she gives the baby a kiss, then you know it is the mother. Similarly, all the "special features" of Krias Yam Suf are the "kiss." Hashem promised Avraham Avinu that He would take us out of Mitzrayim. However, Hashem didn't just want to save us. He wanted to show us extra love. The reaction of the Jewish people to the multitude of miracles that Hashem did for them at Krias Yam Suf was "Zeh Keli V'anvahu – This is my G-d and I will glorify Him." This is the source of the obligation to beautify the Mitzvos and perform them in the most magnificent manner.

**Lesson:** We see from here that if you want to strengthen a bond or relationship with someone, don't just do the bare minimum. Go out of your way to amplify your acts with beauty and meaning and then the recipient will feel the true value of your relationship.

**Source:** Rav Chaim Shmulevitz as cited by Rabbi Goldschmidt

## III. 2016

**Question:** Why didn't Hashem give the Jews the Torah at Har Sinai as soon as they left Egypt after the Red Sea? Why did they first have to receive the Ma'an before getting the Torah?

**Answer:** Rabbi Mendel of Rimanov taught that the Ma'an was a necessary precursor for accepting the Torah. The Torah forbids stealing and coveting others' possessions. It forbids lying, cheating, taking usury and all methods of unlawful enrichment. These laws are in opposition to the innate drives within people. How can people abide by laws that defy innate drives? The Ma'an served as a lesson that a person would get only that which he actually needs. If he had less, Hashem would increase his portion to meet his needs. If he took more than his needs, his greed would result in the excess portion rotting. Once the Jews developed the trust that Hashem would provide for their needs and that accumulating excess was futile, they could accept laws that opposed their natural drives.

**Lesson:** Realizing that Hashem gives us exactly what we need eliminates so many of the negative traits we have (e.g. jealousy, desire to steal, etc.) and serves as the foundation for our life. It is so important, that the Jews had to master this lesson even BEFORE receiving the Torah!

**Source:** Twerski on Chumash by Rabbi Abraham J. Twerski, M.D.

# IV. 2017

**Question:** This week's Parsha has the famous splitting of the sea, followed by the equally famous song, Az Yashir, that Moshe and the Jewish people sang to Hashem. Notably, the posuk says it in future tense: "Az Yashir Moshe U'Vnei Yisroel – then Moshe and the Jewish People WILL SING…" Weren't they singing for an event that just happened in the past? Why does it say they "will sing" in the future?

**Answer:** The Gemara (Sanhedrin 91) explains that this is the song that the Jews will sing at Techiyas HaMeisim (resurrection of the dead). The Belzer Rebbe further explains that Moshe was putting himself in the shoes of many of the Jews' who had just crossed the Yam Suf. Many of them had lost babies during Pharaoh's decree. (Perhaps other lost relatives during the plague of darkness as well, when certain Jews were killed for committing sins). Moshe realized that these people – despite being saved in a miraculous fashion – were still grieving and were sad about their losses. Moshe knew they would not be in a mood to sing and therefore began the song in the future tense, alluding to the fact that they would be singing this together with their relatives during Techiyas HaMeisim. This idea consoled the Jews who were standing there and only then were they able to sing the Shirah.

**Lesson:** We have to be so sensitive to people's feelings, understand what they are going through, and act accordingly.

**Source:** The Power of a Vort, Rabbi Frand, page 125-126

# V. 2018

**Question:** The splitting of the Yam Suf was such an amazing event. Incredible miracles that came with it, such as there being 12 different pathways for the various tribes with transparent walls, fruit being available on the walls of water for children to eat, and a bone-dry ground for them to walk on. In what merit did the sea split? Was it just because Hashem told it to or was there a deeper reason?

**Answer:** Three possible explanations are given, but they all have a common denominator:

(1) **Nachshon ben Aminadav:** Nachshon ben Aminadav was the first one to jump into the Yam Suf. When he saw the Egyptians coming, he jumped in first, even before the sea split. He went against his nature and walked into the ocean, up until his nose! Since he went against his nature of self-preservation, the sea went against its nature and split. Since Hashem saw him take the first step (pun intended), Hashem repaid him – along with the entire Jewish people – in kind.

(2) **Leaving in the Middle of the Night:** The majority of the Jews were living in a city called Ramses when the time of the Exodus occurred. However, there were other Jews scattered throughout Egypt. When it was time to go, these other people left in the middle of the night, when it was more dangerous, just so they could meet up with their brethren. Since the Jews made a monumental effort and self-sacrifice in traveling through the middle of the night – because it is more dangerous to travel during that time – Hashem repaid them in kind by upgrading the miracle at the Yam Suf. Namely, the Jews walked through the Yam Suf at night and then the Egyptians attempted to walk through it the next day. The merit of the effort put forth by the Jews in leaving Egypt at night was proportionate to the time in which the sea split (this is based on Ramban).

**(3) Yosef's Bones:** When the sea saw Yosef's coffin coming, the sea saw a person who conquered his strong desire when Yosef refrained from sinning with Potifar's wife. Since Yosef went against his nature, so too, the Yam Suf went against its nature by splitting! (This is based on Yalkut Shemoni).

**Common Theme**: The common denominator in all these situations is that when the Jews "pushed their boundaries" and sacrificed for the sake of Hashem, they were repaid in kind – with Hashem making miracles for them. While it is true that the Gemara (Brachos 20a) says that these days, we don't have the level of self-sacrifice that the people of that time had – and therefore no open miracles are performed for us – the concept remains true that when a person takes the first step in self-sacrifice, that person will be rewarded by Hashem altering life's situation to help them.

**Lesson:** Sacrifice for Hashem and watch miracles occur!

**Source:** Short and Sweet, pages 165-167

## VI. 2019

**Question:** Right before the sea split, Moshe stretched out his hand over the sea and the posuk says that Hashem moved the sea with a strong wind. What was the purpose of that wind?

**Answer:** The Ramban (14:21) explains that when the Egyptians saw the strong winds, they mistakenly believed that it was the wind that split the sea and not Hashem saving the Jewish people. That led them to chase after the Jewish people and ultimately drown.

**Our Observation:** It is implied from the words of the Ramban that had the Egyptians realized it was Hashem splitting the sea, they would have recognized that Hashem was only doing it to save the

Jewish people, but He wouldn't do it for them! Therefore, it seems that if they made this realization – that Hashem was behind it all – they wouldn't have followed after them and would have survived!

**Lesson:** When we make an effort to see that Hashem is the one controlling the world, it may very well save our life!

# Parshas Yisro

## I. 2014 (Song)

*(tune of "On Top of Old Smokey")*

In this week's Parsha, named Yisro,
He heard about miracles, which everyone should know.

Yisro came, to live with the Jews,
He suggested for Moshe, that judges help and choose.

The Jews came to the mountain, called Har Sinai,
Hashem gave us the Torah, nobody can deny.

Lightning and thunder, smoke and clouds,
Hashem spoke to millions, it was quite loud.

Aseres Hadibros, are the Ten Commandments,
Which include keeping Shabbos, and honoring your parents.

The lesson we learn, from the tenth commandment,
Don't be jealous, learn to be content.

## II. 2015

**Question:** The posuk says (19:2), "And Israel encamped there, opposite the mountain." Rashi points out that the word "Vayichan" is in the singular. But why is that, especially since the Torah was describing the encampment of millions of Jews?

**Answer:** Rashi explains that at this particular encampment, the Jewish people were united, "as one man, with one heart." Upon arriving in the desert of Sinai, they put an end to all quarreling, cleansing their hearts from all ill will, and they shared a deep love for one another.

**Lesson:** A prerequisite to getting the Torah was everyone getting along!

**Source:** http://www.aish.com/tp/b/1-min-vort/239888911.html

# III. 2017

**Question:** Yisro had 7 names (see the Artscroll Bal HaTurim, page 715, note 6 for a listing of them). Why is he known as Yisro and not by any of his other names?

**Answer and Observation:** Perhaps it is based on the fact that Yisro made the right decision to no longer serve idols and instead, to become a Jew. In fact, the Bal HaTurim hints at how this is all in Yisro's name. The Gematria (numerical value) of Yisro (616) equals "HaTorah" (616) and also equals the phrase "Komer Hayah L'avoda Zara – He was a priest to serving idols" (616). The Bal HaTurim says that Yisro first served idols and then made the decision to convert and keep the Torah. This is alluded by the Gematria in his name. Perhaps we can suggest based on this Bal HaTurim that because the name Yisro contains the hint for how he made the right decision is precisely why we call him by this name.

**Lesson:** Hashem (and everyone else) will remember you by the decisions that you make!

# IV. 2018

**Question:** How many names did Yisro have and what meaning is there behind his names?

**Answer:** Rashi (18:1) explains that Yisro had seven names. He was called "Yeser" (meaning "extra" or "more") because several verses were "added" to the Torah and credited to him. Specifically, the verses (18:21) that refer to Yisro's advice in suggesting that Moshe appoint additional judges to lighten Moshe's heavy load of responsibilities. The letter "yud" was added to "Yeser" when he converted to Judaism, a recognition that he had changed and was now performing Mitzvos. Rashi further continues and explains that another one of Yisro's names was "Chovav," coming from the word "Chovev – love," because Yisro loved the Torah.

**Our Question:** Out of all seven names, why is Yisro the one that he is most commonly known by? Further, it would seem to be more logical to name this Parsha after his other name Chovev, referencing his love for the Torah, especially considering this Parsha contains the revelation of Hashem at Har Sinai when he gave the Jewish people the Torah. Why wouldn't the Parsha be named "Chovev?"

**Our Suggested Answer:** Perhaps we can suggest that the usage of the name Yisro – both in the manner in which he is commonly known and the name for the Parsha – is an indicator that the underlying reason for that name (e.g., his advice/help to Moshe) is more precious to Hashem than his other qualities, such as his love for the Torah. When Yisro saw that Moshe was struggling to keep up in his judicial responsibilities, Yisro empathized with Moshe, understood his enormous burden, and offered a solution in an attempt to help. Perhaps this quality of seeing another person's struggles and then acting on it by offering help and solutions is more precious to Hashem than even the love for the Torah! And perhaps that is the reason why, out of all his names, we know him as Yisro and name the Parsha as such.

**Lesson:** Pay close attention to another person's pain and struggles and then act on it by offering help and solutions!

*Level 3 and Beyond!*

# V. 2019

**Question:** The opening posuk in this Parsha (18:1) tells us that Yisro heard what Hashem did for Moshe and for the Jewish People. Why does the Torah list out Moshe separately from the Jewish People? Isn't Moshe included in the Jewish People?

**Answer:** The Ramban answers that Yisro heard two separate examples of Hashem's wonders, kindness, and benevolence: one involved what Hashem did for Moshe personally and another example was what Hashem did for the Jewish people as a whole. In the first example pertaining to Moshe, Yisro observed that Hashem allowed Moshe to make demands of Pharaoh, including telling him the plagues were coming, without fearing retribution. In the second example pertaining to the Jewish people, Yisro observed that Hashem took out the entire Jewish nation from Egypt.

**Our Observation #1:** It is interesting to note that the Ramban says Yisro viewed these examples as a "wonder, kindness, and benevolence" – especially the example involving Moshe personally. One might have thought that since Hashem instructed Moshe to speak to Pharaoh, it would be expected that Moshe would not be fearful of any retribution – after all, Hashem Himself told Moshe to do this!

**Our Observation #2:** Furthermore, in regard to the second example, Hashem promised Avraham many years earlier that the Jewish nation would be redeemed from Egypt – so this should have been expected too! Yet you see that no matter how much you "expect" Hashem to give you, a person must always view it as "wonders, kindness, and benevolence."

**Lesson:** If a person makes the effort to realize that Hashem does not actually "owe them" anything and truly looks at their gifts with a kindness from Hashem, they can reach the level of Yisro, who changed his entire life around to get closer to Hashem!

**Source:** See Artscroll translation of Ramban 18:1 and specifically notes 52 and 53.

# Parshas Mishpatim

## I. 2014 (Song)

*(to the tune of "Take me out to the ball game...")*

Mishpatim has many decrees,
Mitzvos are fifty-three,
Eved Ivri gets respect,
Do not treat him like a wreck,

Mitzvos Bein Adam LeChaveiro,
Be sensitive to your fellow,
If you hurt, damage, or don't tell the truth,
It will be tooth for tooth.

Other Mitzvos include,
Eating Kosher food,
The Jews said Naaseh Venishma,
40 days Moshe learned Torah.

Yehoshua, Chur, and Aaron stayed,
With the Jews who prayed,
Learn from all of these Mitzvos and subjects,
Respect other's objects.

## II. 2015

**Question:** Parshas Mishpatim discusses many monetary laws, including if one lends money, it is required to be interest-free (22:24). After detailing broad laws of slavery, injuries, and damages, why would the Torah choose to mention a law that would only apply to some people? Further, what's wrong with charging interest? If someone can't use their money because they lent it, don't they deserve to be reimbursed for that loss?

**Answer:** Our first clue is Rashi pointing out that this is one of only three times in the Torah that the word "Eem" doesn't mean "if," but means "when." This now clearly tells us that it's not just a possibility that money will be lent, but it's a requirement to lend money, whenever possible. Rabbi Chaim Shmulevitz further explains that when someone does an act of kindness, such as lending, it should be without anticipating reward. Mixing a good deed with personal gain can confuse us into thinking that we're doing something because it's right and proper to do, while in fact we're really motivated by the profits derived by doing it.

**Lesson:** The Torah is illustrating that Mitzvos and Chesed should be pure and untainted, without even a doubt of its motivation.

**Source:** Rabbi Chaim Shmulevitz, as cited by the Weekly Dvar (Rabbi Shlomo Ressler)

## III. 2016

**Question:** If a Jew steals and has no money to pay back his theft, he is sold into slavery by the Beit Din. His term lasts six years, at which point he is a free man. If he doesn't wish to go free, he must go through a procedure that involves getting his ear pierced. Following the procedure, he is a slave until the Yovel, the Jubilee Year. Rashi explains that specifically the ear is pierced as a punishment for having heard at Har Sinai that Hashem prohibits stealing, and nevertheless proceeded to steal. Why is his ear punished for a theft which was performed by his hands?

**Answer:** The Sfas Emes and Rav Tzvi Pesach Frank answer that had he properly "heard" the prohibition against stealing, he would have internalized the lesson and been unable to subsequently transgress. The fact that he was able to violate this commandment reveals that at the time that he heard it, it went "in one ear and out the other," (pun intended!) and for this disrespect toward Hashem's Mitzvos, the ear indeed deserves to be punished!

**Lesson:** Listen to Hashem's messages properly! We can practice this by listening and paying attention to other people when they talk!

**Source:** Rabbi Ozer Alport

# IV. 2017

**Background:** The first posuk of the Parsha has five Hebrew words, which, when translated, mean, "These are the laws that you shall place before them," of course referring to all the laws that are about to be explained in the Parsha between man and his fellow man. The Baal HaTurim says that when a judge makes a true judgment, it is as if he kept the entire five books of the Torah (which he says is alluded from the fact that the posuk has five words, corresponding to the five books of the Torah). The Baal HaTurim continues and says that in addition, this person is also considered as if he was a partner with Hashem in the creation of the world!

**Question:** The judge simply made the right decision. Why is he given so much credit that he is considered as if he kept the entire Torah and that he is a partner with Hashem in the creation of the world? Isn't that a bit extreme? Furthermore, while it makes sense that the Baal HaTurim explains the correlation between the five words in the posuk and the five books of the Torah, why does he continue on to say that it's as if the person is a partner with Hashem in creation? That last part seems superfluous?

**Our Suggested Answer:** Perhaps the Baal HaTurim is teaching us a lesson in the power of Emes – truth. When a person renders a truthful decision, it's no small feat. Sometimes it may not be the popular decision. Other times, it might even run contrary to common sense. But being truthful is that important to Hashem. Perhaps that's why the Baal HaTurim explains that a judge rendering a truthful decision has such a special status – to emphasize how important this trait really is in Hashem's eyes.

**Further Support:** In fact, Pirkei Avos (1:18) says that the world exists because of three things (truth, judgment, and peace) and one of them is Emes – truth! This could possibly explain why the Baal HaTurim added the extra line of saying that such a person is considered as if he was a partner with Hashem in the creation of the world!

**Lesson:** Being truthful may be hard sometimes, but if we remember the special status that it comes with – being considered as if you kept the entire Torah and were a partner in creation – it may help motivate us to tell the truth!

**Source:** See Baal HaTurim, Artscroll edition, page 759

# V. 2018

**Background:** When the Jewish people accepted the Torah, they said "Naaseh V'Nimsha – we will do, and we will listen." When the Jewish people said this, a Bas Kol (Heavenly voice) came out and said, "Who revealed the secret of the angels?" As if to say that the Jewish people had latched onto something special (Shabbos 88a).

**Question:** What secret did the Jewish people identify and what was so special about the manner in which they said these words?

**Answer:** The Zera Shimshon explains that when work is done because a person was *told* to do so, it is not usually performed with as much completeness compared to a person who *wants* to do it on their own, without any pressure. Therefore, when a Jew – who was told to keep the Torah – actually keeps it with completeness and excitement, they will receive even more reward than other people, since it goes against the tendency of doing it just because they have to!

Therefore, the Jewish people were saying that even if Hashem gave them a lesser reward of someone who wasn't commanded to do the Mitzvos (e.g., Naaseh – we will do it without being instructed to do so), they would accept it! The Jewish people were making it clear to Hashem that they wanted to keep the Mitzvos just because Hashem wanted them to – not because of the reward that comes with it. That's why they switched the order of the words, to show that the reward wasn't important to them. They wanted to keep the Torah for the sake of the Torah; not the reward. And that was the secret of the angels – that they don't do their jobs for the reward!

**Lesson:** While it is nice to receive a reward for learning Torah, the real reason to keep the Torah is that it is so special, and Hashem wants us to!

**Source:** Zera Shimshon, Artscroll Volume 1, page 247

# VI. 2019

**Background:** This week's Parsha begins with the Eved Ivri – the Hebrew slave. The classic scenario of this slave is one who stole from a person, didn't have money to pay it back, and then became the slave of the owner to "work off his debt."

**Question:** Does the master have to take care of the slave's wife and children as well or only the slave?

**Answer:** The Ramban says (7:3) that indeed, the master is obligated to take care of the whole family. The Ramban continues to explain that this command is out of the mercy of Hashem for both the wife/children and also for the slave, who could die out of grief for working for someone else while his wife and children are abandoned.

**Observation #1:** Why would the slave die of grief? Wouldn't he realize that his tenure as a slave is limited in time and scope and then be reunited with his family afterward? If there's a light at the end of the tunnel, why would he despair? Apparently, the emotional struggle is so strong that it would override any intellectual recognition that his tenure is limited in time and scope.

**Lesson:** From here you see how careful we have to be with people's emotions, as emotional disappointment and despair can do severe harm.

**Observation #2:** It's amazing that the Torah has to command the master to do this! It is implicit from the Ramban's words that the master would not have taken it upon himself to support the wife and children – he would literally abandon these Jewish people – if the Torah did not command him to do so! Is it possible that a Jewish master would not have mercy? How can this be? It's possible that when someone steals from you and does harm to you (as the slave did to the master to get him there in the first place), a person can become so desensitized that he won't even have compassion and think about the rest of that person's family unless the Torah commands him to do so.

**Lesson:** We see from here how hard it is to forgive someone after they have wronged you, but we have to do our best to move past it and treat them with love and respect.

# Parshas Terumah

## I. 2014 (Song)

*(tune of "If you're happy and you know it")*

Terumah talks about the holy Mishkan,
A place to Daven and to bring a Korban.
The Jews will carry it, anywhere they choose to go,
It will be a special place to learn and grow.

The Aron has the Luchos inside of it,
The Shulchan holds the bread without a mit,
Menorah was quite bold, from one solid piece of gold,
The large Mizbayach made of copper and round polls.

Moshe asked the Jews for their things,
Including gold, silver, and their precious rings,
The lesson that we learn, from the way the people gave,
Learn to give to others and don't just save.

## II. 2015

**Question:** Parshas Terumah is the beginning of the building of the Mishkan, where Hashem would dwell among the Jews as they traveled in the desert. To build the Mishkan, materials had to be collected, and Hashem commanded the Jews to collect several types. After listing the need for metals, wools, hairs, skins, and wood, the Torah tells us that they collected "oil for illumination" and "spices for the anointment oil and incense." Why does the Torah suddenly need to tell us what the materials were to be used for, when it hadn't discussed it thus far? What was so special about the oil and spices?

**Answer:** There is a key difference between the characteristics of the other materials and those of the oil and spices. While the other materials were important, they required no effort in producing, while the oil and spices had to be manufactured and maintained. Those people that didn't have the precious stones to donate to the building of the Mishkan still had the opportunity to contribute with their efforts instead.

**Lesson:** The most beautiful and rewarding things in life are those that require our active effort. Spices smell nice and oil illuminates bright because someone took the time and effort to make them. When we put in the effort to do a Mitzvah or a Chesed for someone, that effort is the biggest treasure of all.

**Source:** Rabbi Shlomo Ressler in his "Weekly Dvar"

## III. 2016

**Question:** The verse states, "The poles (which were used to carry the Aron Kodesh) shall remain in the rings (which held them in place) of the Aron; they must not be removed (Shemos 25:15)." Why shouldn't the poles be removed?

**Answer:** There are different types of Mitzvos. There are those which are applicable at certain times, such as Tzitzis and Tefillin, which can only be fulfilled during the day. There are other Mitzvos which are not applicable at all nowadays, such as Korbanos (sacrifices). And then there are other Mitzvos which are constant. A person must carry these Mitzvos around with him in his heart all of the time. These Mitzvos are the foundations of Yiddishkeit, and since the Aron Kodesh represented the Torah, these constant Mitzvos, symbolized by the poles, were to never be removed.

**Lesson:** We should be thinking about Hashem all day long. He is the One who created everything and keeps it all running.

**Source:** Rav Levi Yitzchak of Berdichev, see also http://www.shemayisrael.com/parsha/kindertorah/archives/teruma75.htm

## IV. 2017 (Part 1)

**Background:** The Midrash Rabbah says that everyone from the Jewish nation was involved in making the Aron, and by doing so, they had the merit of being attached to the Torah.

**Question:** The Aron was so intricate and was housing the most precious item, the Torah. Presumably, this should only have been built by Betzalel, who was given the specific Siyata Dishmaya (Divine assistance) to build it. What involvement could the regular Jewish people have had in the building of the Aron?

**Answer:** The Ramban explains that each person was encouraged to either (a) donate one gold article for the making of the Ark, (b) assist Betzalel in some supportive way (e.g., carrying his tools), or (c) participate mentally by channeling his thoughts (Kavannah) to the matter.

**Lesson:** In order to be involved with a project, show your support in ANY way, whether it is financial, physically helping, or even just thinking about them in your Tefillah! There's ALWAYS something you can do to help...and by doing so, you will merit to be "attached" to the merits of it!

**Source:** See Artscroll Midrash Rabbah to Terumah 34:2, note 35.

# V. 2017 (Part 2)

**Background:** The Parsha starts off where Moshe is about to approach the Jewish people for money as contributions for the Mishkan. The Baal HaTurim explains (25:1) that the language of the opening posuk indicates that Hashem was telling Moshe to speak to the Jewish people in a gentle, more comforting tone. The Baal HaTurim continues that because Moshe's request involved the expenditure of money, therefore he had to comfort the Jewish people ahead of time.

**Observation #1:** The Jews were experiencing the miracle of the Ma'an – whose entire purpose was to instill a sense that Hashem gives us exactly what we need for Parnasah – nothing more and nothing less. All the miracles surrounding the Ma'an (e.g., if you took more than you needed, it rotted, etc.) were there to emphasize the lesson that we have exactly what we need at all times. One would have thought that the Jews would be learning the lesson from the Ma'an and therefore not be disturbed by Moshe's request for money!

**Observation #2:** The money that the Jews had in the desert originally came from the Egyptians, who gave it to the Jews as they were leaving Egypt. The money was never theirs to begin with and therefore it would be shocking to think the Jews would take offense to part with something that was just given to them!

**Observation #3:** Moshe's request was not for a frivolous purpose; it was to construct the Mishkan, Hashem's holy house! Could anyone possibly be hesitant to part with their money for such an honor?

**Observation #4:** Later on, in the Parshios, we know that the Jews were rushing to bring all of their items to donate to the Mishkan (which is why the Nesi'im were eventually left out, as they waited to see what was missing). This indicates that these were people who were excited and enthusiastic to donate to the Mishkan. If such a passion and enthusiasm existed within them, why would Hashem be so concerned to ask Moshe to speak so gently?

**Lesson:** For all the reasons mentioned above, you see how sensitive we have to be when talking to people about their money. Even when money is given to someone easily or it's for a lofty purpose – or even when that person has a genuine passion to be an Eved Hashem – people are hyper-sensitive when it comes to parting with their money and/or property. But when we approach them from a sensitive and gentle angle, the response can be overwhelmingly positive, as proven from the ultimate result of the Jewish people's contribution to the Mishkan!

## VI. 2017 (Part 3)

**Background:** The Torah talks about the Keruvim that are placed on top of the Aron. The Baal HaTurim writes (25:22) a two-part comment:
> (A) The Gematria (numerical value) of the phrase "Shnei HaKeruvim – the two Keruvim" is 637, which is the same numerical value as "Avraham, Yitzchak, and Yaakov." This, says the Baal HaTurim, alludes to the notion that the Keruvim were there to recall the merits of the Avos.
> (B) The two Keruvim, plus Moshe, represent a threesome corresponding to the three Avos, as hinted from each of the first letters of the words, "M'Ben Shnei HaKeruvim," which spell "Moshe."

**Question:** While the purpose of the first part of the Baal HaTurim discussing the Keruvim and the Avos is understandable, what is the purpose of the second part regarding the corresponding threesome? What connection, if any, is there between the first and second parts of the Baal HaTurim?

**Suggested Answer:** Perhaps we can suggest that the second part of the Baal HaTurim is giving us a formula for how to invoke the merit of the Avos. Indeed, the Baal HaTurim writes elsewhere (25:18) that the Keruvim appeared "as two friends discussing the words of the Torah." With that in mind, perhaps the Baal HaTurim is telling us that when we keep to the Mesorah – namely, a Rebbe (e.g., Moshe) teaching Torah to students, who then discuss words of Torah among each other (e.g., Keruvim) – this is the way to invoke the merit of the Avos!

Furthermore, it is worthwhile to note that the Baal HaTurim specifically uses the word "Chaveirim – friends" when describing the Keruvim, possibly alluding to the fact that the merit of the Avos is contingent on being "friendly" to one another. That means acting with Derech Eretz, proper Middos, and without Sinas Chinam. Only THEN will the merit of the Avos be invoked!

**Lesson:** We see the power of a Mesorah and friends discussing words of Torah between one another! Such a scenario may be so powerful that it invokes the merit of the Avos!

## VII. 2018

**Background:** Rashi (see 25:5 and also 26:15) explains the beams of cedar wood used to make the Mishkan originated from Yaakov many years earlier. Yaakov had Ruach Hakodesh (Divine Inspiration) when he left Canaan. Before he left to Egypt, he saw that in the future, hundreds of years later, the Jewish people would need cedar wood to build the Mishkan. Therefore, Yaakov brought cedar wood with him from Canaan to Egypt, planting it there, and telling his children that when the Jews eventually leave Egypt years later, they should take it with them because they will need it in the desert.

**Question:** Put yourself in Yaakov's position at that time when he was about to leave Canaan. He had been away from his son Yosef for many years, and just found out that Yosef was alive, after mourning his loss for years. While Yaakov knew how much the Jewish people would need the cedar wood, it was not going to be relevant for literally hundreds of years later! Wouldn't the expected reaction of a desperate father to simply drop everything and rush to see his son who he just found out was alive? Why would Yaakov concern himself with dragging cedar wood across countries when it's something that could have been dealt with at a later time? He had hundreds of years to find a solution. Why do it now?

**Our Suggested Answer:** Perhaps we can suggest that this is a lesson in Zerizus and excitement in doing a Mitzvah. We know that a person should never pass up the opportunity to do a Mitzvah. Yaakov knew it was something the Jews would eventually need, and he didn't delay even one minute. He put all of his other personal emotions and logistics aside and decided he would take the opportunity to bring the wood now, as it was a precious Mitzvah. This is how much he valued the Mitzvos. He capitalized on the opportunity when Hashem gave him the Ruach Hakodesh at that very minute.

**Lesson:** Never pass up an opportunity to do a Mitzvah! When you are presented with an inspiring moment to do something, capitalize on it right then!

# VIII. 2019

**Question:** When instructing the Jews to build the Aron Kodesh, the Torah uses the plural word of "they." This is in stark contrast to the Torah's instruction of building the other items of the Mishkan, where the Torah instructs the singular version of "you." Why does the Torah make the change when talking about the Aron?

**Answer:** The Ramban (25:10) quotes a Midrash, which says that since the Aron contained the 10 commandments, Hashem wanted everyone involved in building the Aron. This was in order for them to have the merit of being attached to the Torah. Therefore, the Torah used the word "they" in the plural, indicating that each and every person needs to be involved in its construction. The Ramban elaborates and explains the methods of how a person could contribute to the Mishkan: either through (a) donations of gold/money to make the ark, (b) physical assistance to Betzalel who was building it (e.g., carrying his toolbox), or (c) participate mentally by directing their thoughts to the matter.

**Observation #1:** It's fascinating that a person could contribute to the building of the Aron simply by "directing their thoughts!" Apparently, the power of thinking about building the Ark would attach you to the Torah! This is an incredible lesson in the power of our thoughts.

**Observation #2:** The Torah is telling us that by giving (whether in money, service, or thought), it creates an attachment to the Torah. By extension, if you ever want to attach yourself to any Mitzvah – which often involves other people, such as Shalom Bayis, Bikkur Cholim, helping your children, etc. – you should do so by **giving** to them. By giving to another person, you will merit to develop an attachment and closeness with them.

**Lesson:** The power of just thinking about someone or something will attach us to them! Plus, the secret to attaching yourself to the Torah, Mitzvos, or relationships is to constantly GIVE.

*Level 3 and Beyond!*

# Parshas Tetzaveh

## I. 2014 (Song)

*(tune of "Itzy Bitsy Spider")*

Tetzaveh is a Parsha about the Kohein's clothes,
A shirt, hat, and belt, pants down to his toes,
The Kohein Gadol got extra things to wear,
A coat, apron, and headband, right around his hair.

He wore something special, right around his heart,
The Choshen Mishpat was quite a piece of art,
Twelve precious stones; one for each tribe,
Ask it any question, answers it would provide.

Make a small Mizbayach inside the Mishkan,
The Kohein burns spices, the smell would be quite calm,
The lesson that we learn from the Choshen Mishpat,
Is to always ask advice, don't just trust your gut.

## II. 2015

**Question:** Parshas Tetzaveh contains the Mitzvah to create the priestly garments for Aharon and his sons. The regular Kohein's uniform consisted of four garments and the uniform of the Kohein Gadol consisted of eight garments. One of these eight garments was a breastplate known as the Choshen HaMishpat. Why did Aharon merit to wear the Choshen Mishpat and be the Kohein Gadol?

**Answer:** The Gemara (Shabbos 139) explains that Aharon merited wearing the Choshen HaMishpat on his chest by virtue of the fact that "he rejoiced in his heart" (Shemos 4:14) when he saw his younger brother Moshe return to Egypt as the newly-appointed leader of the Jewish people. Aharon was happy for Moshe and his ascension to leadership.

**Lesson:** Sometimes, when someone else gets elevated instead of you, it's easy to become jealous and upset. But when you are happy for the other person and can rejoice alongside them for the success they are having, Hashem will make sure to reward you accordingly.

**Source:** Rav Frand, see http://www.torah.org/learning/ravfrand/5775/tetzaveh.html

# III. 2016

**Question:** Aharon is told to wear very fancy expensive clothes when he was doing the service in the Tabernacle. He wore 8 different articles of clothing, and the regular priests wore four. And the punishment for not wearing them or for even changing something on one part of the uniform was Kares – death. What is the reason the Torah puts such a strong emphasis on these clothing?

**Answer:** Clothing makes an impact on:
> **(A) The Person Wearing Them**: By getting dressed in special garb to perform the service, the priest is reminded of how important and special this task is. By having heavy garments and a long robe, the priests, and especially the High Priest, will not be able to take their minds off of this lofty job they have.
> **(B) Everyone Else Seeing Him:** If we, the visitors/spectators are meant to take the service seriously and respect it and feel closer to Hashem when watching it, then the scene we see must be impressive. And since we humans are sensory beings, all of the visual stimulation helps us to be awe-struck and inspired when we watch the service.

**Lesson:** Clothes have an affect on your mood and it can also affect how people treat you.

**Source:** http://www.aish.com/tp/pak/fp/48881627.html

# IV. 2018

**Question:** As Purim approaches, we read about Parshas Zachor, which is remembering to get rid of Amalek (Haman was a direct descendant of Amalek). How did Amalek start out? Where did they come from?

**Answer:** The Gemara in Sanhedrin tells us that a girl named Timna went to our Patriarchs to accept her into the "camp" of Judaism, but they rejected her. She then went to Elifaz (son of Eisav) and became his concubine. This union produced Amalek, our eternal nemesis. The Gemara concludes that this was, so to speak, the punishment of the Avos for pushing Timna away. Although the Avos must have had a good reason for rejecting her, Chazal tell us it was an error. We learn from this an incredibly important idea. It is one thing not to go out and bring someone closer to Hashem. It is entirely different to reject someone who comes to you!

**Lesson:** We must always remember that our behavior and demeanor can serve either to attract or repel potential candidates for keeping the Torah and Mitzvos. We need to be sensitive to every person as they explore Torah Judaism!

**Source:** Rabbi Salid, PATH email, on February 23, 2018

# V. 2019

**Question:** The Kohein Gadol wore a total of 8 garments: 4 special garments plus the 4 regular garments that an ordinary Kohein would wear. One of those extra special garments was the Me'il (robe), which had bells at the bottom. What was the purpose of those bells?

**Answer:** The Ramban (28:43) explains that there were two purposes of the bells, which would ring and make noise as the Kohein Gadol was walking into the Kodesh Kadashim (Holy of Holies): (1) to ask "permission" from Hashem before entering the Kodesh Kadashim and (2) to let the angels know they should leave the Kodesh Kadashim. The reason the angels needed to leave was because the angels would want to harm the Kohein Gadol since they are protective of Hashem and do not know if the Kohein Gadol has Hashem's permission to enter there. To protect the Kohein Gadol, the bells sound as he is walking in, so the angels know to leave.

**Our Observation:** When analyzing the two reasons why the bells were needed – to seek permission from Hashem and to inform the angels to leave – one would think that by merely getting Hashem's permission to enter, the angels would have automatically left as a domino effect, realizing that the Kohein Gadol had permission from Hashem to enter. The fact that the Ramban says this second reason was a necessity – a special invitation for the angels to leave – shows that they would not have necessarily left on their own. They needed the extra attention, care, and direction.

**Lesson:** Make sure to give attention to each person directly. When a person realizes you are paying special attention to them and are providing them with custom-tailored advice/direction, they are more likely to listen to you!

**Source:** Artscroll Ramban 28:43, note #176 on page 288

*Level 3 and Beyond!*

# Parshas Ki Sisa

## I. 2014 (Song)

*(tune of "Shoo Fly Don't Bother Me")*

Ki Sisa talks about,
Giving a half shekel,
Betzalel and Aholiav,
Built the Mishkan with much love.

Moshe, went up, to get the first Luchos,
The Jews, miscounted, a golden calf arose,

Jews dancing all around,
Luchos thrown to the ground,
Moshe begs Hashem,
Another chance, please forgive them.

Moshe, went back, to get Luchos again,
He said 13 attributes of Hashem.

The lesson that we learn,
From how Hashem yearns,
Be patient, don't get mad,
Be a trooper and be glad.

## II. 2015

**Question:** The women did not participate in the sin of the Golden Calf. Their reward is the special designation of each Rosh Chodesh as "their holiday" and they, therefore, have a custom not to work on Rosh Chodesh. What is the connection between refraining from participating in the Golden Calf and the celebration of Rosh Chodesh?

**Answer:** Rosh Chodesh represents a new month; a time when a person makes a commitment to grow and improve from prior months. The golden calf represented the opposite mind frame: to remain young (like a calf) for an everlasting time period (like gold, which is permanent). The participants of the Golden Calf didn't want to grow spiritually; but since the women rejected that notion, the holiday of Rosh Chodesh, which represents growth and commitment, became theirs!

**Lesson:** Hashem never wants us to remain stagnant. Continue growing, and each month, look for new ways to make it the best one yet!

**Source:** Sefer "Short and Sweet" page 221

# III. 2017

**Background:** Regarding the half-shekel coin, Rashi cites a Midrash that Hashem showed Moshe the appearance of a coin made from fire weighing a half-shekel and told him "This is what they shall give." Rashi actually abbreviates the Midrash. The Midrash itself mentions that Moshe had difficulty envisioning what exactly the half-shekel coin looked like and Hashem, therefore, showed him a heavenly vision of exactly the way it appears. The coin was made out of fire.

**Question:** The commentators are bothered – why was it so difficult for Moshe to envision the appearance of this half-shekel coin? Why did Hashem have to show Moshe a coin made out of fire?

**Answer:** The Oznaim LaTorah explains that Moshe had difficulty understanding how money could serve as an atonement (Kaparah).

Money is the root of most evil. However, Hashem speaks of the half-shekel donation being "kesef hakipurim – the money of atonement." Moshe wanted to know how that can happen. How could something that is the cause of so much evil and trouble serve to bring man closer to His Maker?

Therefore, Hashem showed him a coin made out of fire. Is fire good or bad? Fire can be the most destructive thing in the world. It can kill. It can decimate. On the other hand, where would we be without fire? We would freeze in the winter. We would not be able to prepare our food. The world would not be able to exist without fire. The point of showing Moshe the coin made out of fire was to equate money with fire. Money, too, can be destructive or constructive, depending upon how it is used.

**Lesson:** We see that there are things in this world that can bring tremendous good and at the same time can bring tremendous evil.

**Source:** Rabbi Frand, see http://torah.org/torah-portion/ravfrand-5770-kisisa/

# IV. 2019

**Background:** In the incident involving the Golden Calf, Moshe observes the mayhem transpiring. On his way down, several conversations take place between Moshe, Yehoshua, and Aaron. Using the Ramban's commentary to the story, embedded in these conversations are a pattern of extreme sensitivity and consideration for feelings. If these were the sensitivities undertaken for one of the worst sins in Jewish history, imagine to what great lengths we should go to when dealing with people for much more sublime infractions! Here's what happened according to the Ramban:

- **Episode #1:** The Ramban (32:18) explains that when Moshe came down from the mountain, he had already been informed by Hashem that the Jews made the Golden Calf.

Yet, when Moshe told Yehoshua about the incident, he simply alluded to it by saying he heard the sound of fun and excitement, without actually mentioning the details of the incident itself. The Ramban explains the reason Moshe only hinted at what they were doing was because Moshe was extremely sensitive to the Jewish people and did not want to talk about their disgrace explicitly. [OBSERVATION: Yehoshua was about to see with his own two eyes exactly what they were doing! Nonetheless, Moshe did not want to explicitly speak derogatorily about the Jews, even though Yehoshua would find out for himself moments later!]

- **Episode #2:** The Ramban (32:21) notes that when Moshe spoke to Aaron about the sin, it would have been proper for Moshe to rebuke Aaron for committing the sin and leading the people down a bad path. But that's not what Moshe did. He intentionally left out criticism of Aaron in his sensitivity of, and out of respect for, his older brother.

  [**Observation:** One would have thought that since this was the worst sin the Jewish nation had ever committed and so much was at stake because of it, Moshe would have at least mentioned it to Aaron in a soft tone. Further, at this point, Moshe broke the tablets and would soon go back again to get a new pair. Any rebuke Moshe would have given to Aaron could have served as constructive criticism so that it wouldn't happen a second time! Finally, one can be sure that Moshe would have said it in an indirect or sensitive manner, but that's not what he did. Moshe didn't mention it at all – because of sensitivity and respect for an older brother!]

- **Episode #3:** The Ramban (32:22) elucidates that when Aaron was explaining to Moshe his defense of what happened, Aaron condensed his words so he would not

*Level 3 and Beyond!*

prolong discussing the Jewish people's corruption. In particular, the exact words that Aaron uses – "I threw the gold into the fire and the calf emerged" – implies that there was a miracle that a calf came out from this pot of gold. But the Ramban explains this was not what happened. Rather, Aaron's intention within these words was to tell Moshe the following: "The calf that I intended for permissible purposes emerged as this golden idolatrous calf – all because of the evil and corruption of the Jews!" But Aaron did not explicitly say how bad the Jews were; he merely hinted to it (by saying "the calf emerged") because he did not want to prolong his derogatory statements about the Jewish people.

[**Observation**: Aaron knew he was in deep trouble and the forthcoming punishment would be harsh. It would have been quite understandable and plausible for Aaron to defend his actions and explain that he had the best of intentions and it was the Jewish people who created the havoc. He would be assisting Moshe and Hashem in extracting justice from those who were at fault! Yet Aaron did not do so because of his sensitivity to the Jewish nation!]

**Lesson:** Each one of these examples speaks volumes about the sensitivity Moshe and Aaron displayed throughout this incident. Criticism and derogatory statements never get us anywhere good. We need to be sensitive to people's feelings, even when others make some big mistakes!

# Parshas Vayakhel

## I. 2014 (Song)

*(Tune of "The Muffin Man")*

Vayakhel starts with all the Jews,
Coming to hear the good news.
Everyone builds the Mishkan,
Shabbos we don't work on.

Thirty-nine types of work,
We don't do for any perk,
Betzalel was the one to build,
But everyone used their skills.

Cutting wood was done by the men,
Women made pretty curtains,
The lesson we learn, from their art skills,
It's just a matter of will.

## II. 2015

**Question:** The Jewish People had to be restrained from bringing any more gifts, donations, and jewelry to the Mishkan. Why were they stopped? The Beis Hamikdash was actually more lavish, so why not let the Jews bring even more donations to the Mishkan to make it as beautiful as possible?

**Answer:** The Menachem Tzion explains that since the Mishkan was portable, the Leviim had to carry it from place to place, and Hashem didn't want it to be too heavy for them. Therefore, the Jews were not allowed to bring any more donations, since extra items would have made it harder for them to carry.

**Lesson:** We must always be careful to consider the feelings and hardships of another person, even when we are performing a Mitzvah.

**Source:** Sefer "Short and Sweet" page 233

# III. 2018

**Question:** The Midrash Rabbah says (Vayakhel 48:3) in addition to the Jewish people, animals also assisted in building the Mishkan. How is this possible? How did animals participate in building the Mishkan?

- **Answer #1: Animals came on their own:** The animals whose fur and hides were used for the Mishkan (e.g., to make the covers and dye) came on their own to the Jewish people, ready to offer themselves. The people did not need to go into the wild and look for them. (Chidushei HaRim)

- **Answer #2: People without skills became talented handymen:** The Midrash is alluding to the people who didn't have any craftsman skills. Similar to animals who do not have a knowledge base to build, even the people without those skills were able to participate in building the Mishkan. (Eitz Yosef)

- **ANSWER #3: All people had natural instincts on how to build:** The Midrash is referring to the fact that just as animals were born with natural instincts to function and survive (e.g., birds know how to flap their wings and fly without being taught), so too, all the Jewish people had natural instincts in how to build the Mishkan. (Rav Simcha Bunim of Pshishcha)

**Our Observation:** The common denominator between all 3 answers is that the holiness of the Mishkan elevated everyone around it. Whether it was animals, unskilled people, or everyone who suddenly obtained natural instincts, there was a certain Siyata Dishmaya (Divine Inspiration) given to those around the Mishkan. It elevated them beyond their normal capabilities. The animals went against their normal tendency and came on their own, the people who were not talented suddenly became skilled craftsmen, and everyone miraculously had natural building instincts more than usual.

**Lesson:** We all have obstacles and challenges in our lives. But if we surround ourselves with Kedusha and Torah – such as learning in a yeshiva, going to shul, and associating with Talmidei Chachamim – we will receive special help from Hashem and be given Siyata Dishmaya to go beyond our normal capabilities. Just as everyone around the Mishkan was catapulted to greater levels, we hope the same will be true for us!

**Source:** See Artscroll Midrash Rabbah, Vayakhel 48:3, see page 3

# Parshas Pekudei

## I. 2014 (Song)

*(tune of "Rain Rain Go Away")*

Pekudei starts with a count,
Of gold and silver of all amounts,
The Mishkan is now all complete,
Building it was a special treat.

Make Bigdei Kehunah,
The 8 clothes of great awe,
Aharon the Kohein Gadol,
Knew Torah was the goal.

Hashem's cloud covered them,
From the Mishkan, it would stem,
Learn a lesson from the count,
Other's money there was no doubt.

## II. 2017

**Question:** The half-shekel tax was used to produce the "Adanim," the sockets that formed the foundation of the Mishkan, as the wooden planks/beams were implanted in these sockets. (See the Artscroll book on the Mishkan, page 203 for a visual image of them). We are told that there were 100 Adanim (sockets) in the Mishkan. Why 100?

**Answer:** Just as the Mishkan had 100 Adanim, so too says the Baal HaTurim (38:27), every person should make 100 Brachos every day.

**Rochel's Observation**: Perhaps the connection between the sockets and Brachos is that both help "connect" things: the sockets allow the beams to connect in place and Brachos help us connect to Hashem. By being grateful and thanking Hashem with each Bracha, we are then able to connect to Him in a very real way.

**Additional Idea**: The Targum Yonason Ben Uziel explains that when you say "Modim anachnu lach," if you concentrate on the word "Modim" which is the Gematria (numerical value) of 100, it's as if you said 100 Brachos every day.

**Lesson:** The Mishkan, which represented Hashem's world, where He lived, was held up by the 100 Adanim. And our world should be held up by the 100 Brachos that we say every day. It should be the foundation of our world by thanking and recognizing Hashem 100 times every day, helping us connect to Hashem!

**Source:** Rabbi Yechiel Spero on March 22, 2017

# III. 2019

**Background:** The Ramban (39:42) notes that in regards to the construction of the Mishkan and its vessels, the Torah mentions that the Jewish people built the **tools** themselves first, followed by the building of the actual Mishkan. The reason the Torah did it in this order (e.g., tools first) was to teach us that the Jewish people were careful in making the tools – something considered low on the priority scale compared to the Mishkan and its vessels – and they did it exactly as Hashem commanded them. They gave the tools the care and dedication that it deserved.

**Question:** It seems unusual that the Jews wouldn't make the tools with the same level of dedication and care, especially when considering:

(a) The Mishkan represented the fact that Hashem forgave the Jews for the sin of the Golden Calf, one of the worst sins in Jewish history. Wouldn't the Jews have given priority to everything associated with it, including the tools?

(b) We know that Pirkei Avos tells us to treat a "small" Mitzvah with the same respect as a "big" Mitzvah. Didn't the Jews know this and therefore would make the tools with a great deal of care?

(c) Hashem Himself commanded them to make the tools – wouldn't that be a good enough reason for them to treat it with care and concern?

**Answer:** Apparently, the urge to dismiss the "small" things is very real. People naturally focus on the "bigger" and "flashier" Mitzvos and even the Jewish people had a hard time grappling with it. They overcame their natural desire to put the tools on a lower scale and instead gave it the care and attention it deserved.

**Lesson:** Focus on the "small" Mitzvos and "small" acts of Chesed just as carefully as the "big" ones!

# Parshas Vayikra

## I. 2014 (Song)

*(tune of "Old McDonald had a Farm")*

Vayikra starts with Hashem calling, Moshe in the morning.
Now that the Mishkan was all ready, presents would be many.
Five types of Korbans; for everyone,
Here a Korban, there a korban, go get a special one.
Only bring what you can afford, Hashem will not ignore.

Korban Olah, Mincha, and Shlamim, it's your choice.
Chatas and Asham you must bring, in a committed voice.
The lesson that we learn, from the Korbanos,
Olah, Mincha, it doesn't matter,
Every present you bring to Hashem, is a special gem.

## II. 2015

**Question:** Regarding the types of animals that can be brought as Korbanos, there are only 2 types of acceptable birds, and one of them is the pigeon. What is so special about pigeons?

**Answer:** The father and mother pigeon stick together. They will never leave one another. Even if the father pigeon dies, the mother pigeon will not associate with another male pigeon. This loyalty is the relationship we profess to have with Hashem.

**Lesson:** Always be faithful to Hashem.

**Source:** Little Midrash Says, page 10

## III. 2017

**Question:** The posuk tells us that the Korban Chatas (sin offering) was slaughtered in the same place as the Korban Olah (burnt offering). Why are both the Chatas and Olah slaughtered in the same place?

**Answer:** The Chizkuni explains that the reason we placed those who brought the Chatas with those that brought Olah, is because we wanted to save the sinner from embarrassment. Therefore, if the person bringing the Chatas would stand with the one bringing the Olah, no one would know who the sinner is and who is bringing the Korban Olah in the regular course of business.

**Lesson:** We see how far the Torah goes to make sure the sinner is not embarrassed! We should also do the same to make sure we don't embarrass people.

**Source:** Chizkuni, quoted by Rabbi Spero in Inspiration Daily on March 29, 2017

## IV. 2018

**Background:** As we start Sefer Vayikra, the Torah lists the various Korbanos that are to be brought. The Torah begins by telling us the ones that are voluntary (e.g., Olah, Mincha, Shlamim), followed by the ones that are required (e.g., Chatas and Asham). Indeed, Rashi points out that the Torah progresses from ones that are voluntary to ones that are required (see Rashi 1:2).

**Question:** Wouldn't it make more sense for the Torah to start off telling us what is required and then inform us what is voluntary? Why start with optional Korbanos?

**Our Suggested Answer:** Perhaps we can suggest an answer based on some classic Mefarshim that explain Korbanos:

- Rav Samson Raphael Hirsch explains that the root word of Korban is "karev – to come close," meaning that the whole purpose of Korbanos is to get close to Hashem.
- The Kli Yakar explains that the posuk (1:2) can be translated as, "If a person brings of himself a sacrifice to Hashem" – meaning we can sacrifice a part of ourselves – through fasting and a broken heart.

Perhaps we can suggest, based on the explanations above, that if the whole point of the Korbanos is to get closer to Hashem, it's possible that a person who brings a **voluntary** Korban is more likely to be closer to Hashem than one who is **required** to bring one. By the very nature of things, when a person does something on their own, they feel more attached and committed to the cause – which is precisely the purpose of the Korbanos. Therefore, perhaps Hashem listed the voluntary Korbanos first, to teach us that those are the ones that likely have the hallmarks of what a Korban is all about.

**Practical Application:** The Shulchan Aruch says that these days, when we don't have the Beis Hamikdash, our Tefillos take the place of the Korbanos. In a similar manner to what we described above, we see how important it is to approach Tefilla from the perspective of connecting to Hashem. Not just something we do because we have to, but because of something we want to do and get closer to Hashem.

**Lesson:** Use davening as an opportunity to get closer to Hashem. Don't just daven because you have to, but rather talk to Hashem throughout the day because you want to!

**Source:** See the Sefer "Welcome to Our Shabbos Table," pages 177 and 184

# V. 2019

**Background:** Sefer Vayikra starts off with Hashem calling Moshe and telling him about the Korbanos. The Ramban (1:1) quotes the Chachamim who say that Hashem called out Moshe's name by saying "Moshe, Moshe!" every time before Hashem spoke to him. This applied not only to commands but also to the Dibros ("speaking") and Amiros ("sayings"). Essentially, no matter what Hashem was telling Moshe, He always began by calling his name. The Ramban explains that Hashem did this to show Moshe love and encouragement.

**Question #1:** We can understand Hashem showing Moshe love and encouragement when commanding him; everyone needs additional motivation right before they are asked to do something. But why would Hashem feel it's necessary to exert extra time and effort in motivational techniques when He is simply talking to Moshe through "sayings" and "speaking?"

**Question #2:** Isn't the mere fact that Hashem talked to Moshe enough of an encouragement and sign of love? Nobody else in the Jewish nation had this privilege! Why did Hashem deem it necessary to explicitly show love and encouragement when it was self-evident from the mere communication itself?

**Question #3:** Why did Hashem find it necessary to call his name each and every time a conversation would start? Wouldn't it suffice to do it at the beginning of the relationship, and after a handful of times, cut to the chase and get right down to business?

**Our Suggested Answer:** Perhaps the answer to all these questions shows a critical psychological concept in human relationships —

people need an overabundance of love and encouragement. There is no such thing as "too much" motivation. Human beings crave feelings of love, respect, appreciation, and encouragement. And no matter how many times it's showered upon a person, it is never enough. That's why Hashem showered love and encouragement on all communications with Moshe (not just commands), did it explicitly, and did it consistently all the time. And if this was the case for Moshe, we can only imagine how necessary it is for us!

**Lesson:** In all our relationships, we need to show people constant love and encouragement, through all of our communications. And remember, there's no such thing as "too much!"

# Parshas Tzav

## I. 2016

**Background:** Unlike the other Korbanos that are brought mainly for Hashem, a Korban Shlamim is brought when a person wants to have a feast but also wants to include Hashem. The meat is divided between Hashem, the Kohanim, and the owner, and all this meat will be eaten over two days. The Korban Todah is a kind of Korban Shlamim, but it differs in that it must be consumed the day it is brought and before the next morning. Also, there are 40 loaves of bread that need to be consumed during this short period.

**Observation:** Rav Shimshon Pincus explains the reason for these differences. The Korban Todah is not just any feast, it is a feast of gratitude to Hashem for a salvation you received. It is not enough to be thankful in private, you must very publicly thank Hashem. It is an opportunity to extend the greatness of Hashem to others and it should not be missed. The strict time limit for finishing the meat and the great abundance of bread means that the host will need to invite many people to his party in order to finish it.

**Lesson:** When it comes to saying thank you to Hashem, make sure you do it properly!

**Source:** http://revach.net/parshas-hashavua/quick-vort/Parshas-Tzav-Rav-Shimshon-Pincus-Korban-Todah-A-Very-Public-Thank-You/3594

## II. 2017

**Background:** Tzav discusses various Korbanos and amongst them is the Korban Todah – the thanksgiving sacrifice. In the future, after Mashiach has arrived, all Korbanos will be dismissed with the exception of the Korban Todah, which will still be functioning. A Korban Todah was brought when a person experienced salvation from a potentially dangerous situation.

**Question:** Once Mashiach comes, there will be peace and tranquility. Under such circumstances, how will there arise a situation from which a salvation will be necessary?

**Answer:** During the times of Mashiach, we will see the "bigger picture" and come to understand that what appeared to be a situation of pain and sadness, in reality, was truly a circumstance of valuable fulfillment. With this realization, in retrospect, every experienced calamity becomes a salvation and therefore a fitting circumstance to bring a thanksgiving offering! One day we'll be saying thank you for the difficulties of life.

**Lesson:** Although it is hard to internalize it when difficult situations occur, we need to remember that they are actually for our benefit, and one day, we will be bringing a Korban to say thank you to Hashem for them!

**Source:** R' Ezer Pine, quoting Otzros HaTorah

# III. 2018

**Background:** Chazal tell us that one of the ten special miracles that were performed in the Mishkan and Beis Hamikdash was that rain never extinguished the fire on the Mizbayach. It continued to burn even as the skies opened up and poured rain down it.

**Question:** Why was this miracle necessary? Why did Hashem cause it to rain over the Beis Hamikdash, only to have a miracle showing the fire on the Mizbayach was not extinguished? Couldn't Hashem have just caused it not to rain altogether?

**Answer:** Rav Chaim Volozhiner explains that a person must always remain steady in his service to Hashem and not give in to any disturbances that might interfere with his service to his Creator. Even when a person will get "rained" upon by whatever the circumstances may be, he must never allow those disturbances to "wash" away his passion for the Torah. Interestingly enough, rain ("Geshem") refers to materialism ("Gashmiyous") while fire ("Aish") refers to the Torah (since Torah is often compared to fire). Therefore, the message the Torah is conveying is that a person must never let the materialism – the rain of this world – overtake the fire and passion of a person's Avodas Hashem, which should burn bright and never be extinguished by the rain!

**Lesson:** Sometimes, we get lost in the hustles, challenges, and materialism of life, to the point that it hinders our Torah growth. We must never let the fire of the Torah be extinguished.

**Source:** Torah Tavlin on March 21, 2018

# IV. 2019

**Background:** When the Kohein (6:4) was to remove the ashes from the Mizbayach, the Torah talks about how the Kohein would remove and change his clothes from the ones he was wearing when offering the sacrifices, so as not to get the nicer clothes dirty from the ashes.

**Background:** The Chachamim note that while the Kohein would always be wearing the Bigdei Kehunah, there were superior and inferior qualities of the Bigdei Kehunah. The superior Bigdei Kehunah would be worn when offering the sacrifices and the inferior Bigdei Kehunah would be worn when removing the ashes.

**Machlokes Between Rashi and Ramban:** According to Rashi, changing clothes was optional (not an obligation) since it would not be proper Derech Eretz to get the nicer clothes dirty from the ashes. This differs from the Ramban, who says it is an obligation to change clothes!

**Our Observation:** One could make the argument that the ashes are still part of – on a much smaller scale – the holy service of offerings since they were the remnants of a Korban that was brought. With this logic, one could argue that it should not be such a "big deal" whether the clothing gets changed (since it's all related to the service of Hashem anyway!) and therefore should be optional to change clothes, as Rashi explains. The fact that the Ramban contends it is an obligation to change clothing out of Derech Eretz and respect shows to the extent we must go when it comes to Mitzvos.

**Lesson:** Be careful in showing the greatest respect for every small aspect of a Mitzvah!

# Parshas Shemini

## I. 2014 (Song)

*(tune of "Three Blind Mice")*

Parshas Shemini,
Starts with a decree,
Presents to Hashem,
Everyone brings them.

Nadav and Avihu went inside,
The Kodesh Kadashim was what they eyed,
They made a mistake and then they cried.
And Aaron obliged.

Animals are Kosher,
If they chew over and over,
With split toes,
Everyone then knows.

A Kosher fish must have fins and scales
Kosher birds have specific details,
The lesson from the Chasida bird,
Chesed is always heard.

## II. 2015

**Question:** Nadav and Avihu were the greatest Tzadikim right after Moshe and Aharon. They even had the best of intentions. They wanted to bring an "extra" gift to Hashem on the inaugural day of building the Mishkan. They knew that out of all the Korbanos, the Ketores (incense) was the holiest and that the most treasured place in the Mishkan was the Kodesh Kadashim. They only wanted to bring "the best" to Hashem. If they were such great people and had such wonderful intentions, what was their mistake and why were they punished so severely with death?

**Answer:** Their main mistake was that they did not consult or ask the advice of anyone – not even each other. Had they spoken to Moshe, Aharon, or even each other for advice, they would have come to realize it was wrong to do.

**Lesson:** Asking advice is very important, even when you have the best of intentions. In all aspects of life, you should ask advice from Rabbeim, teachers, and peers.

**Source:** The Little Midrash Says, page 68

# III. 2016

**Question:** Why does the Torah stress that it was the eighth day of the setting up of the Mishkan? Why is the number of the day given such prominence, to the extent that even the name of the Parsha stresses it?

**Answer:** The Torah wants to teach us that the preparations one makes for doing a Mitzvah have nearly as much importance as the Mitzvah itself. For example, even though the Seder lasts only a few hours, it can require weeks of preparation, including learning many laws and customs. Thus, the reference to the "eighth" symbolizes that the seven days which preceded the consecration, even though they were not the ultimate raison d'etre of the Mishkan, they had importance nearly equal to that of the days that followed.

**Lesson:** One might think it is a waste to spend all that time preparing for such a short event. In reality, however, the preparations are part of the Mitzvah because without them it would be impossible to do the Mitzvah properly.

**Source:** http://www.anshe.org/parsha/shemini.htm

# IV. 2017

**Question:** Why did Moshe build and take down the Mishkan every single day during the first week of the inauguration of the Mishkan?

**Answer:** Moshe was teaching the Jewish people a lesson that often times, a person does not accomplish exactly what they set out to do, but if they keep trying, they will succeed.

**Lesson:** If you fall down, get right back up and you will eventually be successful in your goals!

**Source:** Noam Elimelech, as quoted by the Sefer Torahific, page 68.

**Rochel's Observation:** Perhaps we can also suggest that Moshe was teaching everyone a very important lesson in working hard. Hashem cares about all the effort that we put in, not just the final results. So maybe Moshe was telling us that Hashem values all the effort that we put in, even when it seems that we are constantly "taking things down" and "putting them back up."

# V. 2018

**Background:** Rashi (10:12) explains that due to the sin of the Golden Calf, Hashem decreed a death penalty for Aharon and all four of his children: Nadav, Avihu, Elazar, and Isamar. However, due to Moshe's davening, Hashem decided that two of the children (Elazar and Isamar) would be saved.

**Question #1:** We know that Aharon was regretful of his sin involving the Golden Calf and he was very concerned about it, as evidenced from early pesukim and Mefarshim. We can assume that he davened that Hashem forgive him and his family. Yet, it is Moshe's davening that is being credited for saving Aharon's two sons. It seems pretty clear from Rashi that without Moshe's davening, Elazar and Isamar would not have survived. Could Moshe's davening really have been that powerful?

**Question #2:** Nadav and Avihu made a mistake and were therefore deserving of death. The exact nature of the mistake is the subject of much discussion among the Mefarshim, but the fact remains that their punishment was finalized due to an act that they committed. By contrast, Elazar and Isamar did not do anything wrong. Wouldn't their righteousness be a factor in their survival? Why is it only Moshe's davening that is credited?

**Our Suggested Answer:** We can suggest that perhaps Rashi is teaching us the power of davening – and specifically davening for other people. We may underestimate our Tefilla, and certainly when it doesn't involve us. We may downplay our pleading to Hashem on behalf of other people, thinking we are not as worthy and/or they are the ones in the situation with more potency to their Tefilla. But from here we see that the davening you do for another person has immense power as well. Moshe's davening was so potent that he literally saved two lives because of it!

**Lesson:** When you meet someone that has an issue, Daven with intensity for them! It could be the trigger that ignites their salvation!

# VI. 2019

**Question:** Why must a fish have fins and scales in order to be Kosher?

**Answer:** The Ramban (11:9) explains that fish that have fins and scales always live in the upper and clearer waters, and as a result, are nurtured by the air that enters the water from above the water. This helps warm the fish's body, which in turn, helps get rid of the extra moisture in their bodies and is healthier for the person who eats that fish. On the other hand, the fish who don't have fins and scales lives deep down in the cold, murky, and dirty waters, where the extra moisture they develop inside of their bodies is dangerous to anybody who eats them. Therefore, in order to protect our health, the Torah says to only eat fish that have fins and scales.

**Our Suggested Mashal:** Perhaps we could use this Ramban as a Mashal (parable) for how to choose our environment and friends. Just as the Kosher fish swims to the top of the ocean where it is clear, warm, and nurturing, so too, we should position ourselves to the "top" and best environment, where the people think with a "clear" Torah mind, are "warm" in their Middos, and "nurturing" to our emotions! If we get close to those people who live a life of Torah, Mitzvos, and display good Middos, we will end up being a "Kosher" fish ourselves – just as the Torah prescribes!

**Lesson:** Make sure to be close to Talmidei Chachamim and friends who are loving, nurturing, and have great Middos!

# Parshas Tazria

## I. 2014 (Song)

*(tune of "Row Row Row Your Boat")*

Tazria talks about a brand-new Mamma,
She brings a present to Hashem and dunks in the Mikvah.

Baby boy gets a Bris when he's 8 days old,
The Mohel comes for this Mitzvah the Jewish name is told.

Speaking Lashon Harah is very very bad,
The punishment is Tzoras for him, it makes him very sad.

He goes to the Kohein, who tells him what to do,
If its Tzoras, he goes away, alone to think it through.

The lesson that we learn, from getting Tzoras,
Use your mouth to say good things, if not it's a big loss.

## II. 2015

**Background:** The Gemara in Shabbos 104 tells us that in the Alef Bais, there is the letter "Peh" and the letter "Peh Sofis." The regular Peh is "closed" and the Peh Sofis has an opening in its shape. This alludes to the fact that there are times when a person's "Peh – mouth" should sometimes be "open" and at other times be "closed." How do we know when is the right time to open or close our mouths?

**Answer:** The Maharal explains that the letter immediately before "Peh" is "Ayin," which stands for "Enayim – eyes." We should look with our eyes and evaluate whether we should open or close our mouth. Reasons to open our mouth include learning Torah, davening, saying thank you, or making someone feel good. Reasons to keep it closed include Lashon Harah, chutzpah, making someone feel bad, or interrupting someone.

**Lesson:** We always need to "look" at the situation in front of us and determine whether we should open our mouth or keep it shut.

**Source:** Shabbos 104b, see http://dafnotes.com/english_dafyomi/shabbos/Shabbos_104.pdf and also Rabbi Wallerstein

# III. 2016

**Question:** When a person would get something on their skin that seemed to be Tzoras, the Torah requires a Kohein to be the one to make the decision whether a person's skin affliction is actually Tzoras. Why did it have to specifically be a Kohein?

**Answer #1:** The Kohanim were spiritual people who taught wisdom to others. They would be able to advise those afflicted to check through their behavior and to correct their faults. They would also teach the person how to pray to the Almighty for help. Moreover, the Kohanim themselves would pray for the welfare of the person. (Sforno)

**Lesson:** This is a lesson for someone who finds that Hashem has sent him an affliction. Find a spiritual guide who will be able to point out areas in which you can improve yourself, ask him for advice on what to pray for and ask him to pray for you.

**Source:** Sforno and Growth Through Torah

**Answer #2:** The Kohein's role in the Jewish nation is to bless the Jewish people, and intrinsic in this is a love for other people. It is only when a person has love for others and blesses them that they are qualified to rule on whether that person has Tzoras. People speak Lashon Harah because they DON'T love others as much. By speaking Lashon Harah, they put others down and raise themselves up. The Kohein does no such thing. In fact, he does the opposite: he loves the people and therefore he is the only one qualified to make the decision.

**Lesson:** It is only when you love someone that you can offer them constructive comments.

**Source:** Heard from Rabbi Avi Wiesenfeld on Torahanytime.com from Parshas Tazria.

## IV. 2017

**Background:** In one of the first pesukim to talk about showing the potential Tzoras to the Kohein, the Torah says (13:3): "The Kohein shall look at the affliction on the skin on his flesh: If the hair in the affliction has changed to white and the affliction's appearance is deeper than the skin of the flesh, then it is Tzoras affliction; the Kohein shall look at it and declare him contaminated."

**Question:** Why does the verse tell us that the Kohein will look at the spot twice?

**Answer:** In order to render a person "impure," the Kohein needs to look – and then look again. To call someone impure is a very big deal and it warrants a second review to ensure it is appropriate. Homiletically, before a person judges another person and "calls him impure," they should go back for a "second look," understanding that passing judgment on someone is not something that should be taken lightly.

*Level 3 and Beyond!*

**Lesson:** Before we rush to judge other people or say bad things about them, we should review the situation again very carefully!

**Source:** Heard from Rabbi Wallerstein on TorahAnytime, Parshas Tazria, on April 27, 2017

# V. 2018

**Question:** When the Torah talks about birds (12:6), it normally says the Tur first, and then followed by the Yonah. Why is the order reversed here in our posuk?

**Answer:** The Bal HaTurim (12:6) explains that it is based on the nature of these birds. The Yonah is only loyal to its mate while it is alive, and as soon as the mate dies, the Yonah will move on and find a new mate. The Tur, on the other hand, will remain loyal to its mate even after the mate dies, and the Tur will never find another mate. Since the woman is only bringing one bird, she should ideally bring the Yonah since the Yonah's widowed mate will eventually find another mate, whereas the Tur's mate will remain alone for the rest of its life. We want to be sensitive to the Tur's feelings, as it will otherwise remain lonely after this Korban. Therefore, says the Bal HaTurim, the Torah said the Yonah first, as the woman should preferably bring a Yonah.

**Our Observation#1:** Despite the Tur's loyalty, one would think it would find comfort in the fact that its mate was being used for a Mitzvah as a Korban! Furthermore, this is a bird we are talking about, and yet we see the sensitivity to the bird's feelings. If this is how sensitive we have to be to animals, all the more so we need to be sensitive to a person's feelings.

**Our Observation #2:** Perhaps we can suggest that it is specifically by a woman giving birth that the Torah instructs her to take one bird. This would be in order to teach the new mother a lesson of sensitivity. Being sensitive and empathetic to a child's feelings is a critical parenting and life skill. Maybe the Torah is teaching the new mother how to start off parenting on the right path. Furthermore, perhaps this is a life skill that the Torah wishes the mother to transmit onto her child and therefore initiates this feeling of sensitivity, to get the mother to imbue the same quality into her new child.

**Lesson:** We see how important it is to be sensitive to another person's feelings!

## VI. 2019

**Background:** When discussing the concept of Tzoras on a house, the Ramban says (13:47) this can only occur during a time period when the Jews conquered Israel and divided up the land among the various tribes and families. Only houses that people knew were definitively theirs could get Tzoras. The reason for this is because it would only be at that point in time that the Jews would have "peace of mind" and feel settled, knowing that the house they were living in was truly theirs. This sets off a domino effect of two triggering events:

- **Trigger #1:** The peace of mind that comes with having your own house triggered the Jews to be able to serve and know Hashem properly.
- **Trigger #2:** In turn, this special closeness of knowing Hashem triggers Hashem's Shechina to protect the houses from Tzoras.

**Observation:** It is clear from the Ramban that without the feeling of "peace of mind," a person cannot adequately serve and know Hashem (which ultimately protects you)! And it is impossible to have

*Level 3 and Beyond!*

feelings of peace of mind and relaxation without Emunah. One may think that you could serve Hashem and know about Him despite feelings of frustration and worry. But the Ramban is teaching us that peace of mind is a prerequisite for even the basic level of knowing who Hashem is!

**Lesson:** If you want to benefit from knowing and serving Hashem properly – which is your protective shield – you need to have peace of mind and serenity, which can only come from having Emunah!

# Parshas Metzorah

## I. 2014 (Song)

*(tune of "Mary Had a Little Lamb")*

Metzorah reminds all of us,
The dangers of Tzoras,
If you speak Lashon Harah,
You need to do Teshuva.

After you stop being mean,
The Kohein will make you clean,
He uses 2 special birds,
He says "Tahor" with words.

Tzoras can also be on the walls
Red or green, spots so small,
Then it goes to clothing and skin,
Instead, speak nicely and grin.

The lesson from the Metzorah,
Don't ever speak Lashon Harah,
It hurts the one who speaks it out,
The listener and the one it's about.

## II. 2015

**Question:** Rashi (14:35) explains that when a person sees Tzoras on his house, even if the person is a big Talmid Chacham and very confident that it is Tzoras, the Torah says that the person should come to the Kohein and say "it seems to be Tzoras." Why does the person have to say "it seems to be...?" Why can't he say it definitively?

**Answer:** Rav Yeruchem Levovitz explains that this is teaching a person how to respond in all situations, even in times when a person is very confident. A person should train themselves to always say "I think that...." or "perhaps..." or "I could be wrong, but I think that..." instead of absolute statements.

**Lesson:** Doing so will keep a person humble and allow them to stay away from confrontational arguments with others.

**Source:** Growth Through Torah, page 263

# III. 2016

**Question:** Before the Jews came to settle in the Land of Israel, the Canaanites lived there. The Canaanites knew that the Jews would conquer the land, so they hid their jewels in the walls of their homes. When some of those houses got Tzoras, knocking down the walls was actually a way that the buried treasure would be discovered. Why did Hashem orchestrate it this way? What lesson is Hashem trying to teach us?

**Answer #1:** Even though things look bad on the outside (e.g., Tzoras on the house), there is really something positive on the inside (e.g., treasure!). This is a true example of a "blessing in disguise!"

**Answer #2:** The jewels hidden in the walls also tell us something about people. Some people seem very negative, like a wall covered with spots. But in fact, there is always something positive and beautiful hidden inside them. The Torah is always hidden inside their soul – like the precious jewels.

**Source:** Chabad story for children on April 13, 2016

# IV. 2018

**Background:** We learn in this Parsha that if the Tzoras is white, the person is impure, but if it is red/black, then the person is pure. The colors of the Tzoras seem to be reversed from what we commonly know as acceptable. By Yom Kippur, white is the color that symbolizes purity/forgiveness of sin and red/black represents the sins of the Jewish people. Why are the colors reversed?

**Answer:** The Zera Shimshon quotes the Gemara (Pesachim 50a; see Rashi there as well), which says that sometimes things appear one way in this world, but are the opposite in the world to come. For example, there may be people who are respected in this world (e.g., "white") – perhaps because they were wealthy – but then in the next world, it is reversed (e.g., "black") and nobody gives them any honor (because despite their wealth, they were sinning). Similarly, there are some people in this world who don't have any special status (e.g., "black"), but are indeed righteous and will shine in the world to come (e.g., "white"). This is why the color of Tzoras is white: it is to hint to the person that he is currently sinning, and if he continues like this, he will be bright in this world, but not the next. As for Yom Kippur, it is an exception to this since the day of Yom Kippur itself is like the world to come, when the white actually represents purity and forgiveness.

**Lesson:** The Tzoras is there to teach a person that if he continues on his path of speaking Lashon Harah, he will only be elevated in this world, but degraded in the World to Come. But if he learns the lesson, he will secure his portion of World to Come!

**Source:** Zera Shimshon, see Artscroll Volume 1, page 346 – 347

*Level 3 and Beyond!*

# Parshas Acharei Mos

## I. 2015

**Question:** The Torah says that the Kohein Gadol (high priest) asked Hashem for forgiveness of himself, his family, and of the nation as a whole (16:17). Why couldn't the Kohein Gadol just ask forgiveness for everyone in general, which would also include himself and his family?

**Answer:** Before we can think about fixing the world, we need to fix ourselves and our immediate surroundings. That's why the order starts with himself, then expands to his family, and finally extrapolates to the entire nation. Furthermore, it is fascinating to note that the word "forgiveness" is only mentioned once, and yet it affects himself, his family and the entire nation. It seems that a single positive action (in the form of forgiveness in this case) can have the effect of improving ourselves, our families, and the entire nation!

**Lesson:** We have to work on ourselves first before we can help other people. However, we should be motivated by the fact that one positive action can have ripple effects on the masses!

**Source:** Rabbi Shlomo Ressler from the Weekly Dvar email

## II. 2016 (Part 1)

**Question:** This week's Parsha talks about the Avoda on Yom Kippur, which is also called "Yom HaZikoron – Day of Remembrance." Why is it called by this alternative name?

**Answer:** It is not only Hashem who remembers and reviews our actions, we must also recall and review our actions, learn from our mistakes, atone, and decide how to avoid making the same mistakes in the coming year. Yom Kippur is not, however, a complete exoneration of our sins; rather it is the beginning of the process leading to true Teshuva and self-improvement.

**Lesson:** We have to "remember" what we did, learn from mistakes, and improve going forward!

**Source:** LilMode U'lilamed (Rabbi Mordechai Katz); see also http://www.anshe.org/2014/parsha-acharei-kedoshim/

## III. 2016 (Part 2)

**Question:** On Yom Kippur, while performing the service in the Kodesh Kadashim, the Kohein Gadol would wear special white linen garments. Whenever he would wear those white vestments or change into his regular vestments, he immersed himself in a Mikveh. One normally immerses when he's in the process of elevating himself. If so, why did the Kohein Gadol immerse himself when he changed back into his regular vestments – wasn't he decreasing his level of holiness by changing back into his regular clothes?

**Answer:** Every good deed is supposed to elevate a person and bring him to new heights. All the commandments you perform should be on a higher level than before. After the Kohein Gadol wore the holy white garments, he became so elevated that even the regular service he performed afterward was on a higher level. The regular service went up a notch and he, therefore, immersed himself before donning his regular vestments.

**Lesson:** In life, a person needs to keep climbing to greater heights. His understanding of Judaism needs to be constantly deepened and not remain stagnant. His performance in Mitzvos and appreciation for prayer should be advancing constantly.

Source: http://www.aish.com/tp/b/1-min-vort/202908351.html

## IV. 2017

**Background:** During the Yom Kippur service performed by the Kohein Gadol, he was required to select two identical goats, then he was to cast lots in order to determine the fate of each goat. One was chosen to be used as a sin offering, to be part of the process of enabling the Jewish nation to obtain national atonement. The second goat was sent out into a harsh wilderness.

**Question:** What can we learn from the way in which this service was conducted?

**Answer:** These two goats were identical. They looked the same, had similar life experiences, had similar qualities, and yet one attained the ultimate accomplishment (being instrumental in obtaining atonement for the whole Jewish nation), while the other was cast away into absolute isolation (symbolic of being guilty). Two people may be in the exact same situation and circumstance, yet one can choose a proper reaction and the other can choose a poor one. It's all up to us!

**Lesson:** We have to make the right choices in life based on the circumstances that we are given.

**Source:** Rabbi Ezer Pine, quoted by Rabbi Michael Glass on May 3, 2017

## V. 2018

**Question:** At the beginning of Acharei Mos, Hashem describes how and through which medium He reveals himself to Aharon Hakohein as he enters the Holy of Holies. "For through a cloud I shall be viewed on top of the cover (of the Ark)." Why does Hashem choose to communicate through a cloud?

**Answer:** Rav Simcha Bunim Berger explains that the answer lies in both the form and function of a cloud. (1) Clouds are essential to the world because they are the vessels that bring rain. Without the clouds and their rain, the earth wouldn't produce life. Therefore, it follows that clouds are an appropriate symbol to represent Hashem's relationship with the world, as Giver and Sustainer of life on earth. (2) While the clouds contain the water that rains down and gives life to the world, those same clouds have no real substance. To the untrained eye, it is difficult to discern where the rain is stored in the clouds, much less from where the rain falls. Clouds have form but relatively little tangible mass. Therefore, Hashem was telling Aharon on the holiest day of the year (Yom Kippur) that (a) He is the one who gives life (just like the cloud gives the rain) and (b) Hashem is involved with our lives even when we look and can't see Him because He is not tangible (like a cloud).

**Lesson:** We have to realize that the source of our life is Hashem and that He is involved with every part of it even when we can't tangibly see Him!

**Source:** Quoted in http://www.torahtavlin.org/wp-content/uploads/2018/04/27-Achrei-Mos-Kedoshim.pdf

# Parshas Kedoshim

## I. 2014 (Song)

*(tune of "Ten Little Indians")*

Kedoshim starts with Hashem saying,
Do holy Mitzvos by obeying,
This includes respecting your parents,
Give poor people presents.

Pe'ah, Leket, and Shichicha,
Farmers listen to these laws,
Do not steal or hurt your friend,
Pay on time – don't offend.

Wool and linen are Shatnez,
Don't wear them, the Torah says,
Leave the Payos by your ears,
Only look like Jewish peers.

Learn to honor older folks,
Be quite kind and don't play jokes,
The lesson of Klal B'Torah,
Ve'ahavta Le'reiacha Kamoacha.

## II. 2015

**Story:** This is a story based on the concept of "Love your neighbor as yourself." There was once a grandmother sitting on a porch with her granddaughter. As they were enjoying each other's company, a large number of butterflies began to surround them. But then all of a sudden, amid the many butterflies, a moth landed on the balcony. The granddaughter, noticing the moth and thinking that it was out of place next to the butterflies, took off her shoe to kill it. But her grandmother stopped her. "My dear child, don't kill the moth." "Why not?" the little girl asked.

"Let me tell you the story of the moth," the grandmother began. "When Hashem first created the world, He made many butterflies. There were no moths which existed. As Shabbat was drawing near, Hashem decided that He would create a colorful rainbow to show the world that He would never destroy it. The only problem was that Hashem had used all the colors up; there were none remaining. So He went to the butterflies and said, "Can you give me your colors so I can make a colorful rainbow?" The butterflies replied, "Hashem, we are not giving You our colors. You gave them to us and we are not giving them back." But then another group of butterflies approached Hashem. "Hashem, You are the Creator of the world. If you want to make a rainbow, we will gladly give up our colors for it."

As the grandmother entranced her granddaughter with the story, she pointed to the moth her granddaughter was about to kill. "You see that moth? That was a butterfly that gave up its colors. There is more beauty to it than the butterfly which has all its colors."

**Lesson:** Everyone in this world is beautiful. Some of us may shine forth like a butterfly and exude magnificent colors, while others may externally seem to be colorless and nothing special. But the truth is that we all shine forth with Divine beauty. Hashem blew into each and every one of us a precious Neshama.

**Source:** Rabbi Zecharia Wallerstein from the written version of "TorahAnytime"

# III. 2016

**Question:** What is it about the Mitzvos in this week's Parsha that make a person turn Kadosh?

*Level 3 and Beyond!*

**Answer:** The majority of the Mitzvos in the Parsha are Bein Adam LeChaveiro – between you and your friend. Love your neighbor as yourself, not stealing, and Kibud Av Va'eim are just a handful of examples. Even Peah, Leket, and Shichicha are about helping put aside money for the poor people. Only when a person treats other people with respect can he be considered a Kadosh.

**Additionally:** Hashem told Moshe to speak to the "entire congregation of the Children of Israel…" Hashem commanded Moshe to state this verse to the entire congregation because the majority of the essentials of the Torah are summarized here. To attain holiness, one need not be isolated and withdrawn; to the contrary, the admonition was stated in an assembly to show that we must learn to sanctify ourselves by behaving properly among people.

**Lesson:** Some people think that treating people nicely is an extra bonus, but we see that it is not true! Treating people properly is the only way to get to the high levels of Kedusha.

**Source:** Chasam Sofer, as quoted in Love Thy Neighbor by Rabbi Zelig Pliskin

## IV. 2019

**Question:** The posuk (19:14) states not to curse the deaf and that you should fear Hashem. Why does the posuk specifically mention cursing a deaf person – isn't it inappropriate to curse any person?

**Answer:** The Ramban explains that the deaf person cannot hear your curses and will therefore not be angry at you. Therefore, most people might be inclined to curse a deaf person since they can't hear and will never get upset. The perpetrator is not afraid of them since the deaf person doesn't know any better. To make sure a person doesn't act in this manner, the Torah specifically says not to curse a deaf person, so that person understands it is unacceptable. And that's why the posuk ends by saying to fear Hashem – because the perpetrator does not fear the deaf person!

**Lesson:** We have to be careful with hurting people's feelings – both those who don't know you are saying it and all the more so people who understand it and will get upset! You should always know it is upsetting to Hashem when anyone is cursed.

# Parshas Emor

## I. 2014 (Song)

*(tune of "Hamalach Hagoel")*

Parshas Emor begins,
The Kohein is holy, he can't touch dead skin,
Immediate family is an exception,
It isn't considered a sin.

An animal, that's a present to Hashem,
No mums, means perfection.
Behave nicely, with good Middos,
A Kiddush Hashem will show.

The Parsha is also about,
Pesach, Shavuos, the Omer we count,
Rosh Hashanah and Yom Kippur,
On Succos, Jews are together.

A new baby, calf or lamb,
Stays 7 days before it's a Korban,
The lesson we learn, from this feature,
Be sensitive to Hashem's creatures.

## II. 2015

**Background:** The Torah allows a Kohein to deal with a Mes Mitzvah (a corpse found lying in the middle of nowhere) when there is nobody else around to bury the person. In fact, the Halacha is that if the Kohein Gadol is on his way to the Beis Hamikdash on Yom Kippur and finds a dead corpse with nobody else around, he has an obligation to respect the dead person, bury them, and forego the service in the Beis Hamikdash on Yom Kippur.

**Question:** Why is such significance placed on burying the dead person, one who will not even know the difference since he is already dead? This is especially puzzling considering the Kohein Gadol:

- Could easily go to the Bais Hamikdash and send someone else to deal with the Mes Mitzvah, which would only be a short delay;
- Is the only one authorized to go into the Kodesh Kadashim on that day and he has been preparing (mentally and physically) for months; and
- Has himself, his family, and the entire Jewish people relying on his Avoda for a Kaparah (atonement) for the entire year.

**Our Suggested Answer:** The Torah is teaching us the importance of respecting another person. Respect of a dead person takes precedence over the most **holy service** of the **holiest day** of the year by the **holiest person** of the Jewish nation, when the lives of the entire nation are at stake!

**Lesson:** If this is how important the Torah feels about respecting a dead person, can you imagine how important it must be to respect a person who is alive?! Respecting people, dead or alive, is more important than the Kohein Gadol performing the Avoda in the Kodesh Kadashim on Yom Kippur!

# III. 2016

**Question:** Rosh Hashanah in Torah law is only one day (Rabbinical law renders it two days) and Yom Kippur is only one day. On the other hand, Succos is seven days. Why is there a discrepancy between Rosh Hashanah, Yom Kippur, and Succos?

**Answer:** Rosh Hashanah is a day of waking us up and Yom Kippur is a day when we confess our mistakes. Succos, however, sets us up afresh to obtain the highest earthly possession: joy and happiness before Hashem. There is only one day each for the mood of Rosh Hashanah and Yom Kippur, yet seven days, a complete cycle of days, for the joyful building of our huts and our appreciation of rejoicing before Hashem.

**Lesson:** The normal mood of one's life should be not a broken feeling, but one of joy and happiness before Hashem.

**Source:** Growth Through Torah by Rabbi Zelig Pliskin, quoting Rav Samson Raphael Hirsch

# IV. 2017

<u>PART 1</u>

**Background:** The individual chosen to be the high priest is called a Kohein Gadol. The reason for this name is because he is greater than others in five things: in physical beauty, strength, wealth, wisdom, and age. In fact, the Baal HaTurim says (21:10) that the "Hay" at the beginning of the word "HaGadol" is the Gematria (numerical value) of 5, referring to these 5 traits.

**Question:** Why did the Kohein Gadol have to possess these traits?

**Answer:** Rabbi Yisrael Pesach Feinhandler explains that the task of the Kohein Gadol is to be the leader of the Jewish people. He brings the most important sacrifices and he enters the Holy of Holies on Yom Kippur. Having such a distinguished position demands reverence from others, and that is gained by his possessing qualities that are valued in their eyes, those of physical beauty, power, wealth, wisdom, and age. These qualities give him the tools to fulfill his task completely.

## *PART 2*

**Background:** In regards to wealth, if a person was found to be the best qualified candidate to be the Kohein Gadol, yet was not the richest of them, his fellow Kohanim gave him wealth and made him rich until he was the richest among all Kohanim! (See Baal HaTurim Artscroll, page 1229, note 37).

**Question:** Why did Hashem make it that 4 of the qualities (e.g., physical beauty, strength, wisdom, age) are "natural" that the person is born with, but the $5^{th}$ criteria (e.g., wealth) is something that could potentially be given to a person by other Kohanim?

**Our Suggested Answer:** Perhaps we can suggest that Hashem is teaching all of us that if you are meant to be the Kohein Gadol, Hashem will give you whatever tools you need, whether you are born with them or whether others have to give them to you. But you never have to worry, as Hashem will provide it for you if it is so destined!

**Lesson:** We should always take comfort knowing that Hashem gives us everything we need. There is no need to put undue stress on ourselves. If a person is meant to have something, Hashem will find a way to get it to them!

## *PART 3*

**Question:** The whole reason the Kohein Gadol is supposed to be rich is because that this status commands power, influence, and admiration by others. However, when some Kohanim give the

Kohein Gadol their own riches, won't that cause resentment amongst the Kohanim instead of admiration?

**Our Suggested Answer:** Perhaps we can suggest that this teaches all of us we have the ability to be truly great and "get over ourselves" if we put our minds to it. Perhaps Hashem is teaching us that while indeed, the natural reaction is resentment, each and every person has the ability to overcome that natural reaction and rise to a special level of Emunah, realizing that the other individual was decreed to be the Kohein Gadol and each person should do their part to help him.

**Lesson:** If we truly internalize the lesson of Emunah and believe that Hashem gives each person exactly what they need, there is no reason to ever feel resentment towards other people, even if we are the ones making them richer at our expense!

# V. 2018

**Background:** Parshas Emor discusses the many laws of the Kohein. There are many restrictions for the Kohein, including no direct contact with a dead body (except for his immediate relatives), marriage to divorcees is forbidden, and they have to be careful in their consumption of Terumah and Kodshim.

**Background:** Chazal tell us that when the Torah says the words "Vayomer" and "Vayedaber," they are both instructions. The difference is that the latter is a harsher type of speech and the former is a much softer type of speech. For example, telling children to make their beds by saying, "Will you PLEASE make your bed?" is "Vayedaber." But when you tell them, "Go take a snack," that is "Vayomer," as they are happy to take it.

**Question:** If that is the case, the choice of words that the Torah uses to begin this portion seems strange. The verse begins, "Vayomer Hashem el Moshe – and Hashem said to Moshe." [Vayikra 21:1].

Since the Torah was giving restrictions – in terms of who they could marry, in terms of what they could eat, in terms of what type of funerals they could go to – we would have expected "Vayedaber Hashem," as Hashem is asking them to give up a lot and we would have expected a harsher type of language. Yet, the Torah employed the much softer expression, "Vayomer." Why?

**Answer:** Rabbi Frand, quoting Rav Moshe Feinstein in Darash Moshe, explains the role of the Kohanim was to be the spiritual mentors of the Jewish people. In order for a person to be an effective leader, teacher, and role model, a person cannot feel that their life is difficult and the restrictions are burdening. Rather, a leader and teacher needs to feel privileged. That is why the Torah uses the language "Vayomer" in a softer tone, indicating that the Kohanim have to feel the sense of privilege and excitement to have the special status they were given.

**Mashal:** Imagine a person who goes to buy a brand new car, with all the new gadgets. As he starts reading the instruction manual, he realizes there are warnings and things that are not good for the engine and can reduce its capabilities and longevity. For example, don't shift into drive or reverse when not completely stopped, otherwise it can damage the engine! He learns that only takes a certain type of fuel and that it needs oil changes every 6 months. At first, he feels this burden of restrictions of what he can't do with the car. After just a minute of thinking about it, he realizes, "I am so lucky that I read the instruction manual and know what to do and what not to do because I'm going to have the car a lot longer! Suddenly, it's no longer a burden, but rather an amazing privilege and opportunity to know the secrets of how it operates. Being a Jew is the same way: our Torah is the instruction manual, and once you realize the "restrictions" are there to help you manage/navigate through life properly, you feel privileged to adhere to it!

**Additionally:** The Rambam (Mishneh Torah, Hilchos Shemittah v'Yovel 13:13) says that anyone who decides to step into a role of Torah disseminator and devote his life to the work of Hashem also has the status of a Kohein or a Levi.

**Lesson:** To be an effective Torah leader, parent, or friend, we must all feel that living a Torah life – with all the restrictions – is truly a "Vayomer" privilege. It may be hard, but we are lucky to have it.

# Parshas Behar

## I. 2014 (Song)

*(tune of "Yigdal")*

Behar is a Parsha,
Beginning with Shemittah,
Year 7 leave the land alone,
It's not yours to own.

Year 50 is Yovel,
Your slaves say farewell,
Give back all the fields you bought, it's just as well.

Hashem told Moshe,
About Onas Devarim,
Don't hurt other people or their feelings.

The lesson that we learn,
Lend to other Jews,
Help them in any way you can, this is great news.

## II. 2015

**Background:** The Torah in Parshas Behar presents the laws that apply to the Yovel year, which was observed every fifty years during the times of the Beis Hamikdash. One of the laws of the Yovel is that all servants would be released. In those times, men who fell into poverty had the option of selling themselves as servants as a means of sustenance. The Torah commands that servants may not be held indefinitely, and on the Yovel year, all servants must be released. Interestingly, when the Torah formulates this command, it emphasizes that with the onset of the Yovel year, the servant returns to his family.

**Question:** Rather than simply state that the servant is set free, the Torah found it necessary to note that the servant returns to his family. Why does the Torah specifically mention that the slave returns to his family?

**Answer:** Contemporary society, to a large extent, views family as a burden that undermines a person's freedom. Society thinks that a good life means being free from responsibilities and obligations, where family life imposes many responsibilities and obligations. The Torah has a fundamentally different understanding of the concept of freedom, teaching that the ultimate freedom is the ability to act the way we are supposed to act – which includes caring for one's spouse, children, parents, siblings, and relatives. The servant does not just go anywhere on the Yovel year; he must go back to his family, where he belongs. Family life is one of the greatest expressions of freedom, and thus the freedom granted by Yovel demands a former slave to return to his family.

**Lesson:** We should embrace the obligations associated with family life and view them as one of our greatest privileges and among the greatest sources of joy and satisfaction that we can have.

**Source:** Rabbi Mansour, see https://www.dailyhalacha.com/WeeklyParasha.asp

## III. 2016

**Background:** Rashi, citing Chazal, teaches that the 70 years of the Bavel exile were punishment, measure-for-measure, for the 70 Shemittah years which the Jews failed to observe when they were in Eretz Yisroel.

**Question:** If the Torah assures us that the crop from the sixth year will be excessively abundant, why would any Jews (especially those in the time of the Bais Hamikdash) fail to adhere to the laws of Shemittah and insist on planting or harvesting during the Shemittah year?

**Answer:** Since the sixth year would be so abundant, one could easily be led astray into believing that the seventh year would be equally (or even more) prosperous. Thus, it required great Emunah to recognize that however attractive the short term gains were, they would disappear quickly, whereas the reward for observing Mitzvos, even though it may sometimes seem long in coming, lasts forever.

**Lesson:** Don't be greedy! Rather, when we see the abundance that Hashem gives us, we should appreciate it, realize it all comes from Him, and listen to the Torah when it says in the next year ($7^{th}$ year), it should remain fallow.

**Source:** Rabbi Dovid Feinstein in Kol Dodi on the Torah

# IV. 2017

**Background:** Behar contains verses that describe the Mitzvah to help one's fellow Jew if he finds himself in a situation of need. The verse reads (25:35), "And when your brother becomes destitute and his arm falters with you, and you shall strengthen him (financially)..."

**Question:** The commentators point out that the verse seems to imply that the "giver" also suffers from a "faltering arm;" his arm falters together with yours. What is the meaning of this? Why does the Torah describe the supporter as also in need of help?

**Answer:** The Torah is telling us the required mindset of a true giver: he should empathize with the plight of the person in need whom he is helping. He is best equipped to perform the Mitzvah of giving charity if he can feel the pain and sorrow of the recipient of his generosity. He needs to feel as if his arm is also faltering.

**Lesson:** When someone else is in pain, don't just help them, but feel their pain as well!

**Source:** Based on the Ben Ish Chai, as quoted by R' Ezer Pine

# Parshas Bechukosai

## I. 2014 (Song)

*(tune of "Yigdal")*

Parshas Bechukosai is the last Parsha,
Time to make a Siyum for Sefer Vayikra.
Listen to Hashem and keep the Mitzvos,
Rewards and Brachos will engross.

You'll get lots of food, have peace and families,
Hashem will be with us, making it a breeze.
But if you don't listen, Hashem will get upset,
We will get punished, that you can bet.

A farmer counts his flock, one-tenth goes to Hashem,
A present is quite fitting, appreciate your gems,
The lesson that we learn, from giving Maaser,
Hashem gives us everything; He couldn't be nicer!

## II. 2019

**Background:** The beginning of the Parsha tells us that if a person keeps the Torah and Mitzvos, Hashem promises plenty of blessings, including plenty of rain/food (e.g., Parnasah/money), peace in the land, and no wild beasts to harm us. The Ramban notes (26:6) that although the posuk seems redundant when talking about living in peace, he explains that the first part of the posuk refers to a Bracha for internal peace – that "no man shall wage war against his brother" – whereas the second part of the posuk is referring to a Bracha that no external enemies will bother the Jews (e.g., anti-Semitism).

*Level 3 and Beyond!*

**Question:** When analyzing the plethora of Brachos that one will receive for keeping the Torah/Mitzvos – including plenty of money, elimination of anti-Semitism, and removal of attacks from wild beasts – it's hard to imagine there would be in-fighting among Jews that would require a separate Bracha. Further, the language of the Ramban – that "no man will wage war against his brother" – seems a bit extreme. One can understand annoyances and mild friction between Jewish brethren, but is "waging war" a possibility between Jews, especially when so many other things are going well for them?

**Our Suggested Answer:** Perhaps we can suggest that the Ramban and the Torah are teaching us just how hard it is to get along with people. People have a myriad of complex personalities, character traits, desires, and emotions, and, if left to the natural order of the world without any Brachos from Hashem, it would be challenging, if not impossible, for everyone to live peacefully, even internally within our own nation. We, therefore, need the extra Bracha from Hashem that we should live in peace with each other.

**Lesson:** Be cognizant that due to the complexities of human emotions, it is very hard to get along with people and we therefore need a Bracha from Hashem to help us navigate relationships so there is internal peace even among the Jewish people!

**Source:** See Artscroll Ramban, page 809, footnotes 10 and 11

# Parshas Bamidbar

## I. 2014 (Song)

*(tune of "Jake and the Neverland Pirates")*

Bamidbar starts with Moshe counting all the Jews with glee,
Yo ho! Yo Ho!
Let's go! Let's Go!

The Mishkan traveled with the Jews surrounded by Levi,
Yo ho! Yo Ho!
Let's go! Let's Go!

Each tribe will get their own flag,
They will have pictures that appear.

Join the Kohein,
And the special Leviim,
Kehas carried the holiest of gears,

Aron – Ahoy!
Shulchan – Ahoy!
Menorah – Ahoy!
Mizbayach – Ahoy!

Yooooooo Yo ho! Yo Ho!

Kohanim bring special presents
Leviim brought the Mishkan,
They sang a special tune,

Let's go!

*Level 3 and Beyond!*

The lesson we learn from the counting,
We're all unique and special – each and every Jew.

Yo ho!! Let's Go!

## II. 2015

**Question:** This Parsha starts off with counting each one of the Jews. What lesson can we learn from the counting of the Jewish people?

**Answer:** When Hashem commanded Moshe to count the Jewish people, each person got special attention from the greatest leader of the Jewish people (Moshe) and from the Kohein Gadol (Aharon)! Hashem's message was that the Jewish people are His children; each one is equally beloved and possesses a spark of holiness. Thus, no one should ever feel that they are insignificant.

**Lesson:** Each person is unique in their own way and we always have to know that we are all special to Hashem.

## III. 2017

**Question:** The Torah gives instructions on how the Jewish people should encamp in the desert; on which side of the Tent of Meeting shall each tribe camp and which tribes shall encamp together. The Torah states, "The tribe of Yisaschar...the tribe of Zevulun..." Usually, the Hebrew letter "vov" (meaning "and") is added to the name of each tribe as it is listed. However, the "vov" is conspicuously missing between the names of the tribes Yisaschar and Zevulun. What is the Torah coming to teach us?

**Answer:** The Baal HaTurim explains that the tribe of Zevulun worked to support itself as well as Yisaschar so that the tribe of Yisaschar could totally devote itself to Torah study. They are therefore considered as one tribe and the reward for the Yisaschar's Torah study is the same for both tribes. Yisaschar were outstanding Torah scholars, who often lacked sufficient time to earn a living to support their families and Zevulun were successful merchants, who used their wealth to support Yisaschar's Torah study. Each of their efforts was indispensable to the others' and their reward was the same.

**Chiddush:** Rabbi Chaim Shmuelevitz commented on this that just as one has the merit of Torah study for those he supports, likewise, if one influences another to study Torah, he shares in the merit of that person. We should, therefore, help the study of Torah both through our financial support and through encouraging others to learn!

**Our Observation:** In regards to the Baal HaTurim's explanation cited above, he quotes two pesukim, one of which seems generic in its terminology, and another posuk that specifically refers to monetary support. Perhaps the reason the Baal HaTurim cited BOTH pesukim is for one to refer to money and the other to refer to other types of supporting Torah, such as influencing a person to learn, as indicated by Rav Chaim Shmulevitz.

**Lesson:** Supporting Torah in any way is an incredible investment. Even by encouraging and influencing another to learn Torah, you get tremendous credit and reward!

**Source:** LilMode U'lilamed (Rabbi Mordechai Katz), quoted by http://www.anshe.org/parsha/bamidbar.htm

# IV. 2018

**Question:** Why is Parshas Bamidbar almost always read on the Shabbos before Shavuos?

**Answer:** Parshas Bamidbar starts with Hashem counting the Jewish people. Each and every Jew was counted, irrespective of his background or level of observance. This was to show that every Jew is important and every Jew has a role to play. As we approach Shavuos and accept the Torah, there are some people who feel that they are not worthy enough. "Who am I? What do I have to offer?" They despair and feel that they have no role in the Torah. Along comes Parshas Bamidbar with the counting of each and every person, to remind everyone that Shavuos is indeed relevant to all of us.

**Lesson:** Every person has a part in the Torah!

**Source:** Rabbi Michael Glass quoting Rav Moshe Feinstein

# Parshas Naso

## I. 2014 (Song)

*(tune of "We went to the Animal Fair")*

Naso tells us when,
Gershon carried curtains,
Merari took the wooden boards,
The Mishkan they restored.

Viduy's what we say,
If we stray away,
We ask Hashem to please forgive,
We promise not to relive.

The Nazir leaves his head,
No wine or touching the dead,
Kohanim bless each special Jew,
Hashem guards over you.

Leaders of each Shevet,
Bring 21 presents,
The lesson from Shevet Levi
Res-pon-sib-ili-ty!

## II. 2015

**Question:** Other than carrying the wooden beams and curtains, what job did the Leviim have and why was it so important?

**Answer:** Some Leviim were tasked with guarding the Mishkan, but other Leviim had the job of singing and playing musical instruments

*Level 3 and Beyond!* 169

while the Korbanos were being brought. This was important because the music and singing caused the Jews to serve Hashem with happy spirits. Hashem wanted to ensure that the Jews were not just bringing the Korbanos, but doing so with Simcha!

**Lesson:** Doing the Mitzvos is not enough; we have to do them with Simcha and happiness!

**Source:** The Little Midrash Says, page 37

## III. 2017

**Background:** Parshas Naso begins with the instruction to "count also the family of Gershon" [Bamidbar 4:22]. Levi had three sons – Gershon, Kehas, and Merari. The Daas Zekeinim M'Baalei HaTosfos point out that the counting of the family of Gershon was done by the family of Gershon themselves! Moshe just asked them to give him a number. The family performed a self-census and gave the tally back to Moshe, but Moshe himself was not involved in the counting.

**Question:** Why was the counting of the family of Gershon done by the family of Gershon themselves, different from everyone else?

**Answer:** Gershon was the eldest son. The first-born always receives the preeminent position. He receives a double portion of his father's inheritance. He is the Bechor. He always has special importance. However, among the sons of Levi, the family of Kehas had the most significant duties. This was the family that was assigned to carry the Aron and the other vessels of the Mishkan. Gershon did other things, but the second born received the preeminent assignment, not the first-born.

As the Abarbanel points out, this was somewhat of a slight to the Bnei Gershon. The Abarbanel says that even though Hashem had His reasons for giving the Bnei Kehas the more preeminent role, it is still necessary to take into account the feelings of the first-born. He must be compensated with some sort of a "consolation prize." It is necessary to make him feel good, in spite of the fact that he has been slighted.

The Abir Yosef explains this is why the counting was done by the Bnei Gershon themselves rather than "through the hand of Moshe," as was the case with the other families of Levi. This was to compensate them for the "slight" of having their first-born status bypassed in the distribution of assignments. It is telling them "you have a special status, you have special integrity. We will trust you to count your own family members and report back to Moshe without requiring Moshe to go around to your tents." This too was in order to make them feel a little better.

**Lesson:** We see how sensitive we must be to everyone's feelings!

**Source:** Based on Rabbi Frand explanation of Abir Yosef, Abarbanel, and Daas Zekeinim

## IV. 2018

**Question:** The end of the Parsha contains the recitation of the various sacrifices offered by the Princes of each of the Tribes on consecutive days in honor of the dedication of the Mishkan. Every Prince brought exactly the same offering. How did this happen? Why did they all bring the same Korban?

**Answer:** The Midrash relates that the Nasi from Yehuda was Nachshon ben Aminadav. He was the first one to make an offering and had it easy. He could offer whatever he desired. The second Nasi, Nesanel ben Tzuar of the Tribe of Yisaschar, was faced with a dilemma of what to bring. Should he bring the same offering or something different? The Midrash explains that Nesanel ben Tzuar decided to bring the exact same one because he was concerned that if he tried to be something different than Nachshon ben Aminadav, then the prince after him would follow suit in making his even "better" and it would turn into a contest of who can outdo the other! Thinking ahead, Nesanel ben Tzuar realized it would be a contest among 12 tribes and everyone would argue that his offering was better, leading to Lashon Harah, hatred and jealousy!

**Lesson:** We always need to act in a way that will keep people together and eliminate jealousy and arguing!

**Source:** Rabbi Frand

# V. 2019

**Background:** The Torah instructs various members of the Levi family regarding their tasks in what to carry for the Mishkan. Specifically, the Torah requires that for the Merari family, each person – by specific name – must be instructed to carry a specific vessel, such as planks, pillars, etc.

**Background:** The Ramban (see 4:32) explains that the instructions had to be explicit and specific to each person – and not generally to the family – since there was a concern that due to the heaviness of the items, an individual would remove his load and put it on the shoulders of someone else! Therefore, when providing instructions, each person had to be named and tied to a specific task. The Ramban concludes by saying this was applicable to the Kehas and Gershon families as well.

**Our Observation:** It was a unique and special privilege to carry the Mishkan vessels. For there to even be the thought among some people that they could shirk the responsibility to someone else means that when it comes to bearing a heavy load, there is no shortage of rationalizations. Even when it comes to the holy Mishkan, people can rationalize shirking responsibility (e.g., saying "the load is too heavy"), just to "get out" of a tough assignment. If the Leviim were susceptible to such a mindset, we could also fall prey to that dangerous mentality.

**Lesson:** When doing any type of work – especially Mitzvos – don't be so quick to avoid responsibility, as Hashem may have assigned it especially to you!

# Parshas Beha'alosecha

## I. 2014 (Song)

*(tune of "She'll be coming around the mountain when she comes")*

This week's Parsha is Beha'alosecha
Aharon lights the lamps of the Menorah,
Pesach Sheni is a second chance, for those who were impure,
They were happy to serve Hashem, that's for sure.

People were complaining about the Ma'an,
They didn't thank Hashem for what He had done.
Miriam spoke about her brother, saying Lashon Harah,
She got Tzoras and then a Refuah.

The Jews traveled in the desert with Mishkan,
Hashem's cloud flew away when they were done,
The lesson we learn from the Parsha, from what Miriam thought she saw,
Don Lekaf Zechus; it's the law!

## II. 2015

**Question:** After Miriam spoke Lashon Harah about Moshe, Hashem punished her with Tzoras on her skin and she had to stay outside of the Jewish camp for 7 days until she was clean. During this time, the cloud of Hashem did not leave the Mishkan and the entire Jewish nation. Over one million people waited for her before moving on to their next trip. Why did everyone have to wait for Miriam?

**Answer:** Hashem commanded them to wait for her because of Middah Keneged Middah. Years earlier, Miriam waited by the Nile River watching her baby brother Moshe float away in a basket. She was concerned about him and wanted to make sure he was safe. Since she was concerned about someone else (even her own brother), Hashem recognized her Chesed and therefore, as a reward, caused the entire Jewish people to wait for her.

**Lesson:** Hashem remembers all of the Chesed that you do for other people. And when you show how much you care for other people, Hashem will make sure that other people show their care for you.

**Source:** The Little Midrash Says, page 96

## III. 2017

**Background:** The Gemara in Shabbos (22b) explains that the purpose of the Menorah's light in the Mishkan was to show the entire world (even the non-Jewish nations) that Hashem rests His Shechina among the Jewish people. As Rashi on that Gemara explains, there were equal amounts of oil placed in each of the seven lamps of the Menorah and while the western lamp was lit first, all the other lamps would go out by the morning time, yet the western lamp would burn longer than all the others! It would last until the evening time when the Kohein had to extinguish it and re-light all the others. It was a miracle for all to see! [See Baal HaTurim Artscroll edition, page 1445, note #7.]

**Question:** If there were no windows in the Mishkan and non-Jews could never go into the Mishkan, how would the non-Jewish nations ever know about the light and miracle of the Menorah? How would they know that Hashem's presence rests with the Jewish people if they never actually saw these miracles?

**Our Suggested Answer:** It's possible to suggest that the Jews were so proud, excited, and enthusiastic about this miracle that they talked about it with others, including their non-Jewish neighbors. By the

Jewish people enthusiastically explaining what transpired with the Mishkan to the non-Jewish nations, the entire world would come to realize the special relationship Hashem has with the Jews.

**Lesson:** When we act and talk in a special way among our non-Jewish neighbors and make a Kiddush Hashem, they recognize how special we are and that Hashem's Shechina rests with us. Perhaps this is one of the reasons why we are called "Ohr Lagoyim - a light unto the nations" – referring to the light of the Menorah, which was to do exactly that! We can each be the "Menorah" to light up the world and let the other nations know about Hashem.

## IV. 2019

**Background:** The Ramban states (8:4) that Moshe is regarded as having made the Menorah because he "exerted effort in learning how to make it and he commanded the artisans in charge to make it."

**Observation #1:** When reviewing the wording of the Ramban, the word "Nishtadel –effort" stands out. The Ramban could have easily omitted that word and the explanation would have still made plenty of logical sense: Moshe learned how to make the Menorah and ordered the right people to do so. The fact that the Ramban includes this word "Nishtadel" implies that had Moshe not exerted effort in doing so, it's possible that he would NOT have been credited with building the Menorah.

**Observation #2:** In a similar manner, it's possible to say that had Moshe not exerted the effort, the artisans would not have listened to his command! Perhaps his example of exerting effort was the *reason* the artisans listened to him!

**Lesson:** When it comes to Torah and Judaism, it's the effort that counts in Hashem's eyes!

# Parshas Shelach

## I. 2014 (Song)

*(tune of "Five Little Monkeys")*

Shelach has Jews who want to go,
To see if Israel has a glow,
Moshe sent 12 spies called Meraglim,
They brought giant fruit and wanted to scream.

Two of the spies knew to behave,
Their names were Yehoshua and Kalev,
Trust Hashem, be strong and brave,
You won't get punished; you'll be saved.

When baking bread, take off a piece,
Kohein gets Challah for his feast.
The lesson we learn from Tzitzis,
Do the Mitzvos with a kiss.

## II. 2015

**Background:** The Mitzvah of Tzitzis exists so that a person will look at them and remember to do all 613 Mitzvos.

**Question:** How do the Tzitzis themselves allude to this?

**Answer:** The Midrash Tanchuma notes that the Gematria (numerical value) of the word "Tzitzis" is 90 (for the first "Tzadi") + 10 (for the first "Yud") + 90 (for the second "Tzadi") + 10 (for the second "Yud") + 400 (for the "Tuff") = 600. Then add 8 for the number of threads on each corner of the garment + 5 for the number of knots on each thread. This equals a total of 613, a direct connection to the whole point of wearing them!

## III. 2016

**Background:** Moshe added a "Yud" to Hoshea's name because Yehoshua needed protection from the other spies when they were going to speak Lashon Harah against the land of Israel. Moshe took the "Yud" since it is part of Hashem's name (Yuk Kei Vav Kei) and added it to Yeshoshua's name to protect him from such harm.

**Question:** Why didn't Moshe do anything for the other spy, Kalev, who was also going to refrain from Lashon Harah? And why not for any of the other spies?

**Answer:** Kli Yakar explains that Hoshea came from the tribe of Ephraim, who was the son of Yosef. Many generations earlier, Yosef had spoken Lashon Harah about his other brothers, and since speaking Lashon Harah was in the "bloodstream" of Yeshoshua's ancestors, Moshe felt he needed an extra layer of protection.

**Our Observation:** Despite the fact that (a) Yosef lived generations earlier and Yehoshua never actually saw him commit such acts and (b) Yehoshua was a tremendous Tzadik who was Moshe's "star student," nevertheless, Moshe understood that whatever a person does has an impact on their children and stays in the lineage for generations to come.

**Lesson:** Your actions make a big impact even after you leave this world!

**Source:** Little Midrash Says, page 126

# IV. 2017

**Background:** Rashi cites the Midrash Tanchuma to elucidate the juxtaposition of sending the spies to the land of Canaan to the section of Miriam's speaking Loshon Harah about Moshe. Even though Miriam was publicly punished for speaking against her brother, these wicked people who witnessed her punishment did not learn a lesson.

**Question:** How could the spies be expected to learn from Miriam's Loshon Harah? Miriam spoke against a person, while they spoke against a land!

**Answer:** Rabbi Yisroel Ordman, of Telshe Yeshiva in Lithuania, comments that one must acquire the attribute of always seeing the good in everything. A person who finds fault with things (e.g., meals, accommodations, etc.) will also find fault with people. Conversely, a person who always seeks to find the good in anything will also see the good in his fellow man. That is the lesson the spies should have learned: to notice virtues rather than seek out faults.

**Lesson:** We should always look for the positive in every situation!

**Source:** Growth Through Torah, as cited by Rabbi Packouz

# V. 2018

**Background:** When the spies returned back and were about to give their report, the Torah says, "Kalev silenced the nation (13:30)". Rashi explains that he silenced the people in order to get them to listen to Moshe. He began by saying, "Is this all Ben Amram did?" and then showed the people that Moshe did great things for them. By silencing them into thinking that he was going to join them, he disarmed them momentarily. After that brief break, the spies returned to their evil report.

**Question:** Why was the momentary silence worth it if the people were going right back to their complaints a moment later? Moreover, Kalev receives three rewards for this – he is the forefather of Dovid HaMelech, he receives Chevron, and is called an Eved Hashem. Why does he get so much reward for a moment's work – especially work that did not last?

**Answer:** Rav Zilberstein explains that when tempers fly and people get angry, people can develop a mob mentality. By delaying them, even for a moment, the tempers have a chance to calm down. Even though the spies reverted back to complaining, that temporary moment to calm them down was worth lots of rewards!

**Lesson:** When a person is angry, the best thing to do is delay and distract their anger to allow them some time to calm down!

**Source:** Points to Ponder from 5777, see http://www.adathisraelshul.org/e-torah/parsha/81-shlach/775-points-to-ponder-shelach-5777

# VI. 2019

**Question:** Why did the spies suffer such a painful death of dying from a plague?

**Answer:** The Ramban (13:32) explains that it was specifically because they lied (e.g., when they said that the land devours its inhabitants) in their report that they were punished with the painful death through a plague.

**Observation #1:** The spies did not come back with an initial agenda of lying. They started off their report from a factual perspective (even though it was still negative) and it was only once they started receiving pushback from Kalev that they resorted to lying. So the lying aspect wasn't even their main focus, yet that is what caused their horrendous death!

**Observation #2:** There could have been many other reasons the Ramban could have offered regarding why the suffered from a plague. For example, one could have thought that the lack of faith in Hashem, Loshon Harah, or negatively could have warranted such a harsh punishment. Yet, it was lying that caused such a decree.

**Lesson:** There is an extremely severe and harsh punishment associated with lying. This is because truth is the hallmark of what Hashem and the Torah represent. Make sure to always tell the truth!

# Parshas Korach

## I. 2014 (Song)

*(tune of "Frozen")*

Korach was a rich man one time;
from Shevet Levi,
Jealous of Aharon; Kohein Gadol should be me,
Dasan and Aviram were howling side by side,
Couldn't keep it in, they didn't try.

Don't let them win, make others see,
That the bad guys have pure jealousy,
The earth opened and swallowed them,
They were condemned!

Let it go, let it go!
Be happy and adore,
Let it go, let it go!
Jealousy's out the door.
I don't care if they push me away.
Let my Middos go on.
Thank Hashem and start to pray.

Fire came from Heaven,
Burned people that were bad,
Moshe put 12 sticks inside, nobody was mad,
The stick of Aharon came through,
Now everyone surely knew,
No right, no wrong, no jealousy.
I'm free!

Let it go, let it go!

Be happy and adore,
Let it go, let it go!
Jealousy's out the door.
I don't care if they push me away.
Let my Middos go on...

# II. 2015

**Question:** Which two people listened to their wives in this Parsha?

**Answer:** (1) Korach listened to his wife when she told him that Moshe was wrong and was treating Korach unfairly (2) Ohn ben Peles was originally going to join Korach's rebellion. But Ohn's wife convinced him otherwise. When his wife heard of his intentions, she said to him, "Why are you getting involved in this fight? Don't you realize that regardless of who the leader is, you will remain the same ordinary person? Moshe is a holy man, and it is foolish of you to join an attempt to overthrow him."

Ohn listened attentively to his wife and responded, "You are right, but I have already promised them that I will join the rebellion. How can I let him down now?" His wife replied, "I understand your dilemma; leave it up to me and I will get you out of it." She gave him wine to drink and caused him to be drunk, and then put him to bed inside their tent. She then sat at the entrance to their tent with her hair uncovered, a behavior considered immodest for a Jewish married woman. When Korach and his followers came to the tent to summon him and noticed an immodest lady at the entrance, they decided to leave without him. Thanks to his wife's intervention, his life was saved.

**Lesson:** Korach's wife destroyed him while Ohn's wife saved him! The wife can either make or break the husband!

*Level 3 and Beyond!*

## III. 2017

**Question:** Parshas Korach relates the story of Korach, Dasan, Aviram and 250 members of the tribe of Reuven challenging Moshe's choice for Kohein Gadol. The end result was that the 250 members were burned by a heavenly fire, and the three leaders were miraculously swallowed by the earth. From a motive perspective, Korach's actions make the most sense because he felt slighted for not having been chosen himself, and had something to potentially gain by complaining. But why would 250 people follow him to their certain death, with apparently little to gain?

**Answer:** The answer can be found in Rashi, who writes that just as Korach's family camped on the southern side of the Mishkan, so did the tribe of Reuven. The 250 people met their demise simply because they were influenced by their neighbors. This points to the awesome influence that friends, neighbors, and associates have on us.

**Lesson:** The people we choose to surround ourselves with can make the difference between life and death.

**Source:** Rashi, as quoted by Rabbi Shlomo Ressler in Weekly Dvar

## IV. 2018

**Background:** Ohn ben Peles was about to join Korach's rebellion and his wife convinced him not to. She gave him wine, he went to sleep, and she sat by the entrance of their tent with her hair uncovered, knowing that this immodesty would ward away Korach's followers when they came to get Ohn.

**Question:** Why did Ohn's wife specifically uncover her hair? Why not show a part of her arm or leg? What was the message she was sending Korach's followers by uncovering her hair?

**Answer:** Each hair in the head has a separate follicle and no two hairs share the same follicle. Korach and his followers were riddled with jealousy and could not accept Moshe's position. By uncovering her hair, Ohn's wife was giving them a subliminal message: the same way that each hair has its own follicle, so too, each person has a unique job and mission in this world. She was telling them that they needed to understand and accept that Moshe and Aharon were chosen for those roles by Hashem and they had other unique missions that they were supposed to accomplish. Therefore, she chose to uncover her hair to teach them this lesson.

**Lesson:** Jealousy can be removed when we believe that Hashem gave each person a special job and a unique set of talents intended just for them.

**Source:** Rabbi Wallerstein in his TorahAnytime shiur on June 12, 2018

# V. 2019

**Background:** The Ramban notes that Korach was angry at Moshe for his appointment of Elizaphan (Korach's first cousin) as the leader of Kehas and also jealous that Aharon (also Korach's first cousin from a different uncle) was appointed as the Kohein Gadol (see the Ramban on 16:1 towards the end of the very lengthy piece on this posuk).

**Question:** Why didn't Korach contest these appointments when they initially occurred? Why did he wait until now to start a rebellion?

**Answer:** The Ramban answers that up until this point in the desert, nothing really bad happened to the Jews as a nation. Even the incident with the Golden Calf only claimed the lives of those specific Jews involved with that sin. During that time, Moshe davened on behalf of the other Jews and saved them. Moshe had great favor in the eyes of the people up until this point and nobody would have supported a rebellion. Therefore, Korach didn't voice his displeasure at that time.

Now, however, several incidents occurred that shifted the mentality of the Jewish nation. First, when they entered into Paran and complained, there was a fire that destroyed many of the people (see Bamidbar 11:1 - 3). Second, later on, more people died in Kivros HaTaavah (11:33). Third, the incident with the spies occurred and Moshe did not Daven for the Jewish nation in the same capacity as he previously did. As a result, it was decreed that a large percentage of the Jews would die in the desert without entering Israel. Fourth, a special plague killed the ten spies who spoke negatively about the land, which was traumatizing to observe. The Ramban says that it was now, at this point, after these collective incidents, that the mood shifted within the Jewish people, and that Korach believed he would garner support to overthrow Moshe.

**Our Observation:** It is interesting to note that the Ramban states there were several incidents that collectively shifted the mood of the Jewish people. It is implicit from the Ramban's words that had there been only one (or a couple) of these incidents, Korach would not have felt there was vulnerability among the nation. It was only when there was an overwhelming amount of instances and circumstances that he felt the situation was ripe for rebellion.

**Lesson:** We, too, might be able to handle one upsetting situation or circumstance. But the Yetzer Harah waits until there is an overwhelming amount of suffering – one thing after another – to jump in and wreak havoc. When we start to experience trouble in our lives, it might be manageable to stay strong through isolated instances. But when things start piling up, that's when we really need to be vigilant, strengthen our Emunah, and go back to the Torah and Mitzvos as our guidepost because that will be the time we are most vulnerable.

# Parshas Chukas

## I. 2014 (Song)

*(tune of "Goodbye Bucky" from Jake and the Neverland Pirates)*

Chukas starts with a Chok,
Called Parah Aduma,
Even if we don't know,
Mitzvos are still a go.

Miriam went back to live with Hashem,
And there was no water to drink,
Moshe got angry and hit the rock,
Hashem was in total shock.

Aharon said goodbye today,
Elazar his son would lead the way,
Sichon and Og were giants,
Moshe and the Jews beat these bad tyrants.

How do we say goodbye,
To our friends Miriam and Aharon,
How do we say farewell,
To friends like you.
Appreciate your friends, like they're brand new.

We're so lucky!

## II. 2015

**Background:** Moshe was initially afraid of the giant Og because of a Chesed that Og did years earlier. Specifically, Og told Avraham that his nephew Lot was captured by the four and five kings. Because of that Chesed that Og performed, Moshe was afraid that the merit might make him win.

**Question:** How could Moshe have been worried about Og's Chesed? First, Og's Chesed was tainted because his ulterior motive was for Avraham to be killed in battle so that he (Og) could marry Sarah! Second, this was hundreds of years earlier and chances are his merit would be used up by now. Third, Moshe had Hashem's promise that He would protect the Jews on their way to Israel. How could Moshe be afraid?

**Our Suggested Answer:** This is the power of Chesed. Even a Chesed with ulterior motives and performed hundreds of years earlier has incredible power. When we do something nice for someone else, we may think it is just a "good thing to do." But the reality is that Chesed has such power that it can give you such a Zechus that even Moshe could possibly be afraid of!

**Lesson:** Never underestimate the power of Chesed!

## III. 2017

**Question:** The Torah tells us that Moshe hit the rock instead of speaking to it (as he was commanded to do by Hashem). If Moshe had spoken to the rock instead of hitting it, what would this have taught the Jewish people?

**Answer:** Rashi elucidates that if Moshe were to have spoken to the rock and it would have given forth water, there would have been a greater sanctification of Hashem (e.g., a greater Kiddush Hashem) in the eyes of the Jews. The people would say, "If this rock which does not speak and does not hear fulfills the word of Hashem, all the more so should we."

The essence of sanctifying Hashem's name is not merely that someone should be impressed by another person's righteous behavior or to think that a person is acting in an elevated manner. Rather, the key factor is that other people should be influenced to improve their own behavior.

**Lesson:** If you act in a way that causes other people to become closer to Torah and Mitzvos, that is a Kiddush Hashem!

**Source:** Rabbi Packouz on June 26, 2017, quoting Rabbi Pliskin in Growth Through Torah

# IV. 2018

**Background:** In Parshas Chukas there is another Shirah recorded in the Torah: the Shirah of the Well. Just as Parshas Beshalach contains the Shirah that Moshe and the Jewish people sang on the Yam Suf after their miraculous deliverance from the pursuing Egyptian army, Parshas Chukas contains a Shirah as well (Bamidbar 21:17-20). This Shirah was sung in honor of the miraculous "Well" which had accompanied them throughout their 40-year sojourn in the desert.

**Question:** By the Shirah of the Sea, it starts off by saying Moshe and the Jewish people sang it, but by the Shirah of the Well, it simply says the Jewish people sang it. Why doesn't Moshe's name appear in the song about the Well?

**Answer #1:** Rashi quotes a Gemara (Taanis 9a) that states the juxtaposition of the death of Miriam and lack of water tells us that for forty years, the Jews had water in the Zechus of Miriam, who waited for her baby brother Moshe by the side of the water in Egypt. Now that the water had stopped, all of a sudden Bnei Yisroel started to sing Shirah, thanking Hashem for the well that they had for forty years. Why did they thank Hashem only when the water stopped flowing? Rav Chaim Yosef Kaufman explains that the people knew what Miriam had done, but only now that she was no longer with them, did they realize what they lost and had not appreciated. In contrast, Moshe did NOT have to say Shirah because he thanked Miriam every day of his life – for saving his life when he was a baby!

**Answer #2:** Some commentaries explain that the reason why Moshe's name was deleted from this Shirah was that the "Well" served as the only slight blemish on his otherwise impeccable record as the leader of the Jewish people. Since this "Well" was associated with Moshe Rabbeinu's small "slip" (if we can say such a thing), his name is not mentioned in this Shirah.

**Answer #3:** Rabbi Frand quotes the Shemen HaTov that suggests the Shirah of the Sea was sung at the beginning of the Jewish people's journey in the desert and the Shirah of the Well was at the end of this journey. When the Jews were first starting out on their journey, Moshe had to take the lead and instruct them what to do. However, by the end of the forty years, Moshe was so successful at teaching the Jewish people that they took the initiative on their own to sing a song after witnessing a beautiful miracle. The omission of Moshe's name indicates that whereas at the beginning, he needed to instruct them what to do; compared to the end of the journey, where they were doing it on their own!

**Lesson:** There are lessons from each of the answers, but from the third answer, we learn that the job of any leader is to get the followers to take their own initiative after they have been taught. We are all leaders in some capacity. Instructing others is great – but eventually, the best proof that they have absorbed it is if they are doing it on their own!

**Sources:** Rabbi Frand quotes in https://torah.org/torah-portion/ravfrand-5761-chukas/ and Rabbi Kaufman quoted in http://www.torahtavlin.org/wp-content/uploads/2015/06/35-Chukas.pdf

# V. 2019

**Question:** What was Moshe and Aharon's sin involving water coming from the rock?

**Answer:** There are various explanations as to what exactly was the sin. The Ramban (20:8) explains that Moshe and Aharon said to the Jewish People, (20:10), "Shall we bring forth water for you from the rock?" Notice that they used the word "we" – instead of giving credit to Hashem for performing the miracle.

The Ramban notes that this verbiage was different from when Moshe and Aharon previously spoke about other miracles – such as the Ma'an, the 10 plagues, and the splitting of the Sea – where Moshe and Aharon explicitly gave credit to Hashem for performing those miracles. Therefore, since they did not do so in this case, it was possible that the Jewish people would have erroneously concluded it was through the wisdom of Moshe/Aharon – and not Hashem – that brought the water from the rock. This was their mistake. (See Artscroll in-depth elucidation of the Ramban, pages 423 – 425.)

**Our Observation:** It's hard to imagine the Jewish people coming to the wrong conclusion that it was Moshe/Aharon who performed the miracle without the Hashem's help. First, while Moshe/Aharon were utilized as the messengers to perform all past miracles, they never actually performed any miracles on their own! This would have been their first and only time!

Second, after witnessing the fate suffered by Korach and the spies – both incidents that showcased what happens when we fail to recognize Hashem's involvement – one would have thought the

Jewish People would have easily recognized Hashem as the One behind the miracle of water emanating from a rock.

Yet, according to the Ramban, Moshe and Aharon's sin – grave enough to keep Moshe out of Israel – was that they did not explicitly recognize Hashem as the one who was performing the miracle, which would have left it possible for the Jewish people to misinterpret who was in charge.

We are so emotionally fragile that if we fail to explicitly include Hashem in our words and don't give Him credit for all the good happening to us, there is the possibility that we will arrive at mistaken conclusions with dire consequences.

**Lesson:** When you talk about all the good in your life, make it a point to explicitly thank Hashem for it!

# Parshas Balak

## I. 2014 (Song)

*(tune of "Head, Shoulders, Knees, and Toes")*

Balak was a bad king,
Bad King.
He Called Bilaam to do bad things,
Bad Things.

An angel came to stop Bilaam's curse,
The angel talked but it got worse,
It got worse.
Bilaam ignored the Shliach,
From Hashem.

Bilaam tried to curse the Jews,
The Jews.
Instead, his words were misconstrued,
Misconstrued.

Every time he opened his mouth,
Hashem made him say nice things,
Nice things!
The Jews were getting blessings,
Blessings!

Bilaam had a wicked scheme,
Wicked scheme.
Hashem will get upset and scream,
And scream.

Let non-Jewish girls entice them,
Serve idols and condemn,
And condemn.

It worked and many people sinned,
People sinned.
Hashem made them sick and thin,
And thin.

Zimri was a leader who didn't care,
Pinchas speared the evil pair,
Evil pair.

Do the right thing everywhere!
Everywhere.

## II. 2015

**Background:** Balak, king of Moav, had a grandson by the name of Eglon, who had a daughter named Rus. Of course, Rus later converted to Judaism and was the ancestress of King David, and ultimately, the Mashiach.

**Question:** What did Balak, a wicked and evil king who wanted to curse the Jews, do to deserve having Rus, and ultimately Mashiach, descend from him?

**Answer:** The Gemara says "One shall always occupy himself with Torah and Mitzvos, even not for the sake of Heaven, as he will ultimately come to do so for its sake." In the merit of the forty-two sacrifices that Balak offered to Hashem (even though they were intended to help curse the Jews!), Rus descended from him. The sacrifices were offered to gain Hashem's favor so that He would allow Balak and Bilaam to carry out their evil plans. Nevertheless, no matter the intentions, "a Mitzvah is a Mitzvah." Balak had the merit of having offered sacrifices to Hashem and he was rewarded accordingly.

**Lesson:** Even with bad intentions, performing a Mitzvah and serving Hashem has tremendous rewards! Can you only imagine the rewards if we serve Hashem with the proper intentions?

# III. 2016

**Question:** Why would Bilaam, who heard his donkey speak, begin to threaten it with death? Doesn't he realize that a supernatural event is occurring? Further, why would he threaten to kill the animal? By doing so he would never get to his destination. Wasn't that a totally irrational threat?

**Answer:** Bilaam was experiencing the event of a lifetime. He had an angel directly in his path, and his donkey was actually speaking to him. But he did not notice. He had his eye focused on one thing. His heart was set on cursing the Jews and collecting a handsome fee. Miracles were occurring all around him but he lost all rational control. He did not notice. He was only interested in his honor. He would have slaughtered his donkey on the spot.

**Lesson:** The world around us is filled with miraculous events, some of which may even be greater than a talking donkey! All we have to do is listen.

**Source:** Rabbi Mordechai Kamenetzky

# IV. 2017

**Background:** The Parsha has the famous blessing that Bilaam gave the Jews: "Ma Tovu Ohalecha Yaakov..." which means, "How goodly are your tents...."

**Question:** Why does the posuk say "tents" in the plural? What are the multiple tents that this is referring to?

**Answer #1:** The Baal HaTurim explains that Yaakov was both in an earthly tent as well as a Heavenly tent. Therefore, it says "tents" in the plural. (Some people say that Yaakov is referring to the individual, while others explain it is referring to the nation of Israel. Using the latter explanation, the Jewish people have a "tent" in this world [e.g., they live in this world] and also a "tent" in the next world [e.g., they have a share in Olam Habah.])

**Answer #2:** The Baal HaTurim continues and explains that the plural form refers to the six sanctuaries/places where Hashem lives, such as the Mishkan. The Baal HaTurim identifies these 6 future places where there would be a Mishkan (not including the one in the desert): (1) Nov (2) Givon (3) Gilgal (4) Shiloh (5) the first Bais Hamikdash and (6) the second Bais Hamikdash.

**Our Observation:** It is interesting to note that anytime there are multiple answers given by the Baal HaTurim, he usually starts off by saying "Davar Acher – another explanation is..." However, in this particular case, the Baal HaTurim does not do that. Perhaps we can suggest that the reason he does not separate out the answers is that they are, in fact, connected!

Perhaps here is how: The first part of the Baal HaTurim is providing us with the "secret recipe" for how to build a sanctuary, as was evident from the 6 future sanctuaries. The secret is to connect the mundane to the Heavenly (as described in the first part of the Baal HaTurim). It is well known that what made the Mishkan and

Bais Hamikdash special was that they were able to take the most earthly and mundane items (e.g., sacrifices) and turn them into something spiritual (see Rav Pincus in his Sefer on Shabbos, where he explains this concept in more detail). Therefore, perhaps the first part of the Baal HaTurim is telling is how to create Hashem's house in this world (by connecting the mundane to the spiritual), followed by the 6 future places that accomplished this feat.

**Lesson:** All of our shuls and homes are known as a Mikdash Me'at – a small sanctuary, resembling that of the Mishkan and Bais Hamikdash. Using the above explanation, we now know the secret for how to make them into such a special place – it's by elevating everything we do by saying it's for the purpose of Hashem, Torah, and Mitzvos. For example, when we sit down to eat our food, we can turn the simple mundane activity into something spiritual by saying Brachos, Benching, and realizing the food was provided by Hashem!

# V. 2019

**Question:** As Bilaam is on his way to meet with Balak and subsequently attempts to curse the Jewish people, Hashem creates the miracle of the talking donkey. Why did Hashem make this miracle for Bilaam?

**Answer:** The Ramban explains (22:23) that the reason for this miracle was to show Bilaam that if Hashem can open the mouth of an animal that can't speak, certainly Hashem can take away the power of speech and/or cause a person to say something else in its place. The expectation and hope was that Bilaam would infer this from the incident with the talking donkey, realize that Hashem controls everything, and reconsider his decision. Bilaam should have taken the message to heart. That was the reason for the miracle of the talking donkey.

*Level 3 and Beyond!*

**Our Observation:** As Pirkei Avos (5:6) tells us, the mouth of the talking donkey was one of the 10 amazing creations made at the twilight of the very first Shabbos. Clearly, the talking donkey was something very important to Hashem and played an important role in world history. According to the Ramban, the whole point of this miracle was to send Bilaam a sign that Hashem is in control. It's fascinating to realize that Hashem would go to such great lengths for such a wicked person – creating a special phenomenon, unique in the creation of the world – just so that a wicked person, one incentivized by money and fame, would have the opportunity to see Hashem is in control and revert his decision.

If Hashem cares this much about an evil person, all the more so He cares about the Jewish People, who keep his Torah and Mitzvos! It is inspiring to realize how much Hashem cares about those who follow in His ways. Furthermore, if Hashem was willing to show signs to Bilaam who was about to make an evil decision, it is possible and probable that Hashem will show us signs (although not necessarily as miraculous) that He is in control – we just have to keep our eyes open for them.

**Lesson:** Realize how much Hashem loves us and pay attention to the signs in your life where Hashem clearly shows that He is in control of everything!

# Parshas Pinchas

## I. 2014 (Song)

*(tune of "Rock a Bye Baby")*

Pinchas the Levi gets a reward,
Now he's a Kohein who won't be ignored.
Moshe divides the land of Israel,
Tribes and families get a good deal.

Tzalafchad's five daughters were very sad,
They wanted the land that belonged to their dad,
Moshe asked Hashem what he should do,
Hashem let them have it, they said thank you.

Yehoshua the new leader, they would adore,
Bring a Korban, some days there's more,
The lesson we learn from the daughters of Tzalafchad,
Speak nicely and talk like a nice bud.

## II. 2015

**Question:** Moshe prays to Hashem to appoint a new leader over the nation and Hashem appoints Yehoshua. There were plenty of people who were eligible for this position. There was Elazar, Pinchas, and the 70 elders. Why then did Hashem choose Yehoshua as Moshe's successor?

**Answer:** The Torah says about Yehoshua: "A lad, who did not depart from within the tent" (Shemos 22:11). Already from his youth, Yehoshua gave up every comfort to be in the tent of Torah. He was consistent. Whatever it took, he made sure that he was always there.

It was his power of consistency that made him greater than everyone else!

**Mashal:** If you have a pot of water on the stove and you are waiting for it to boil, but every few minutes you remove it, the water will never boil. It doesn't even matter how big the flame is since each time it is removed and returned, the boiling process starts over from scratch. It is only the continuous process of heating which causes it to boil. The flame could be very small and it may take longer to heat up, but as long as it's consistent, it will eventually begin bubbling.

**Lesson:** Consistency in learning Torah and performing Mitzvos is what makes you a leader.

**Source:** http://www.aish.com/tp/b/1-min-vort/212666911.html

# III. 2017

**Background:** In this Parsha, Moshe must now come to grips with a reality that was extremely painful to him. Hashem told Moshe that he will never enter Eretz Yisrael. This message was already delivered to Moshe in Parshas Chukas, but it is only now that the reality and the finality of the message came crashing down upon him. Upon hearing this news, Moshe's reaction is to ask Hashem to appoint a worthy successor to lead the people.

**Question:** Moshe's reaction seems strange. Why wouldn't Moshe immediately beseech Hashem to let Him into Israel? Why does Moshe go immediately to talking about appointing a new leader for the Jewish people?

**Answer:** Rashi says that this demonstrates the praise of the righteous. When their time comes to leave the world, they abandon their own needs and occupy themselves with the needs of the community. Rather than go with his first instinct to pray to Hashem to rescind the decree and let him go into Eretz Yisrael (as Moshe indeed ultimately does as we read at the beginning of Parshas V'Eschanan), Moshe forgoes that urge and his first reaction is to pray for a worthy successor.

**Lesson:** Even when you have your own problems and issues, don't forget to care about the problems of others!

**Source:** Rabbi Frand citing Rashi

# IV. 2018

**Background:** Rashi explains that the daughters of Tzalafchad came to Moshe to ask for their deceased father's portion in the Land of Israel since their father had died without sons to inherit his portion. In tracing the lineage of the daughters of Tzalafchad, the Torah seems to provide redundant information. The posuk says that they were "the daughters of Tzalafchad, son of Chefer, son of Gilead, son of Machir, son of Menashe" and then that they were "from the family of Menashe son of Yosef" [Bamidbar 27:1]. Why was it necessary to emphasize the fact that they descended from Menashe son of Yosef twice?

Rashi asks this question and answers that the emphasis indicates that the love of Eretz Yisrael is genetic. Yosef loved the Land of Israel and insisted that his bones be returned there. This love for Eretz Yisrael ran in his family such that his descendants (Tzalafchad's daughters) insisted that they be given their fair portion in the Land.

**Question:** The wife of the Sfas Emes asked her son (the Imrei Emes) a question on this Rashi: What is the proof that the daughters of Tzalafchad loved the Land of Israel? Perhaps they were just interested in their inheritance as a monetary matter.

**Answer:** The Imrei Emes gave his mother a very good answer. There are two opinions regarding the identity of Tzalafchad. One opinion is that he was the wood chopper who violated Shabbos and was sentenced to death (see Bamidbar 15:32). Another opinion is that he was from the group who tried to force their way into Canaan after the decree of the spies (Bamidbar 14:40).

Either way, Tzalafchad died in Parshas Shelach, prior to the beginning of the decreed 40 years of wandering. His death occurred some 38 years prior to the events in Parshas Pinchas. If Tzalafchad's daughters were interested in their father's estate from a strictly financial perspective, why would they have waited 38 years to ask for it? Inheritance is not limited to land. What about his cattle? What about his other property? Apparently, they were not interested in that.

It was only now when they were on the doorstep of Eretz Yisrael that they came pressing their claim for the inheritance of their father's portion. This is the demonstration of their love for the Land. They were silent regarding the cash and moveable property. However, their inheritance in the Land of Israel mattered greatly to them. They inherited this affinity to the Land from their great grandfather, Menashe son of Yosef.

**Lesson:** Yosef's love for the land was transmitted many generations later – all because of the acts that he did. We see how greatly a person can influence their children and generations to come!

**Source:** Rabbi Frand citing Rashi and the Imrei Emes

# V. 2019

**Background:** In Parshas Pinchas, we see two distinct examples in the Ramban where the Torah shows us how far we must go to respect another person's feelings. These are:

**Example #1:** Moshe takes a census of the Jewish people to determine the portion sizes each tribe would get in Israel. The Ramban (26:57) notes that it seems strange that the tribe of Levi was counted in this census, considering they would not be getting a designated piece of land. The Ramban, in his second explanation, tells us that that the reason the Torah included Levi in the counting was out of respect for them so that they should not feel inferior to the other tribes, especially since they are a special group of Hashem.

**Our Observation:** The tribe of Levi presumably had a healthy self-image, especially considering they did not participate in the sin of the Golden Calf or the sin of the spies and were excluded from slavery in Egypt due to their Torah learning. Additionally, they were spared many of the punishments the other tribes received because of their proper behavior. It is remarkable that despite all of this, Hashem was still concerned about their honor and that they would potentially feel inferior had they not been counted in this census.

**Example #2:** The Ramban (26:59) explains that while the Torah lists out the names of the Kohanim, it does not specifically mention Aharon and his sons. This was intentionally done out of respect for Moshe's honor since Moshe was not chosen to be a Kohein. [See Artscroll's elucidation of the Ramban, notes 168, 169, and 170].

**Our Observation:** It is amazing that Hashem was concerned about Moshe's honor, especially when we know Moshe was chosen to be the leader of the Jewish people. Further, we know Moshe was happy for Aharon when he became the Kohein Gadol! While it would not appear that Moshe had a self-esteem issue, nonetheless, Hashem felt it was not respectful for the Torah to specifically list Aharon and his sons. We see the extent to which we must go to respect people.

**Lesson:** Even when you may not think it is necessary, be sensitive to another person's honor and feelings!

# Parshas Mattos

## I. 2014 (Song)

*(tune of "Ring Around the Rosy")*

When you make a promise,
Keep it and be honest,
Don't sin,
Go to a Beis Din.

Midyanim are the bad guys,
Pinchas was there to advise,
Beat them in their town,
They all fall down.

Take all their pots and pans,
To the Mikvah with your hands,
Now it's safe to eat,
Eat a Kosher treat.

Reuven, Gad, half Menashe,
Went to speak with Moshe,
We want to obtain,
Eiver Hayardain.

The lesson from our Parsha
A promise is a special law,
Your words are priceless,
You'll have success.

## II. 2015

**Question:** When Reuven and Gad assured Moshe that they would join the battle to conquer Canaan, they told him, "We'll build sheepfolds for our cattle and cities for our children here, but we will be armed to go before the Children of Israel until we have brought them to their place." Moshe instructed them to "build your cities for your little ones, and [then] folds for your sheep." Why did Moshe switch the order?

**Answer:** While Moshe was pleased with their intention to join the other tribes in battle, he saw disturbing signs in their priorities, that they mentioned the building of homes for their cattle before homes for their children. Thus, he was reminding them that the well-being of one's children must come before the well-being of one's material possessions.

**Lesson:** We have to remember that our family is the priority and all other money-related endeavors are secondary.

**Source:** LilMode Ulilamed (Rabbi Mordechai Katz)

## III. 2016

**Question:** Hashem commanded Moshe to destroy the nation of Midyan, who sent the women to marry the Jewish men. What about Moav, who hired Bilaam to curse the Jews? Why didn't Hashem ask that Moav be destroyed?

**Answer:** Hashem foresaw that one day down the road, Rus would be born from Moav and she would be a Tzadekes who would have Dovid and Mashiach. Because of her, Hashem said not to harm Moav.

**Lesson:** Sometimes we don't know why Hashem is doing something and we won't even live to see it. But Hashem always has a reason for what He does.

**Source:** Little Midrash Says, page 252

# IV. 2019

**Background:** After the Jewish people conquered the nation of Midyan, they were commanded to take all their spoils, calculate how much money was involved, and divide it among themselves.

**Question:** When the Torah first makes this command, it says (31:26) the people involved with this calculation should be Moshe, Elezar, and the tribal leaders. A few verses later (31:31), when it describes who actually performed the calculation, it only says Moshe and Elezar, with no mention of the tribal leaders. Why doesn't the Torah include them?

**Answer:** The Ramban (31:31) explains that Hashem only commanded the tribal leaders to be present because it was a money matter and Hashem wanted to ensure that nobody would suspect Elezar of taking more money than he was allotted. Therefore, this command for the tribal leaders to be present was an optional invitation. The tribal leaders essentially responded, "Far be it from us to suspect Elezar, who is like an angel of Hashem! We don't need to be there!" Since they trusted him and did not participate in the calculation and division of the spoils, the Torah did not include them in verse 31. It was a testament to how they trusted Elezar to only take his designated amount and did not need to be there to watch over him.

**Our Observation:** While it is a beautiful testament to the tribal leaders that they ultimately trusted Elezar when it came to money, the fact remains that Hashem offered them the opportunity to be present during this calculation for full transparency. When it comes to money matters, human nature makes people naturally suspicious of potential misappropriation. If Hashem was concerned that people would suspect the Kohein Gadol of potential misappropriation from community funds, all the more so people might suspect us of such activities!

**Lesson:** When it comes to money matters involving the community, ensure full transparency and disclosure!

# Parshas Masai

## I. 2014 (Song)

*(tune of "Alef, Beis, Veis...")*

Masai is about remembering each place,
That the Jews went where they built their tents.

Like the Yam Suf, or Hor HaHar,
Time to enter Israel,
Bad guys there would steal,
Don't be like them, tell them you condemn.

Each tribe gets a piece of Holy Israel,
Except for a few tribes, they were described.

Killing someone else, even by accident,
Is never ever ok, now you have to go away,
To an Ir Miklat,
Be aware, always love and care.

## II. 2015

**Question:** In describing the journeys of the Israelites during their forty years in the desert, the Torah not only enumerates the various resting places but at each point states, "They traveled from A and camped at B. They traveled from B and camped at C, etc." Since the Torah doesn't even have a single superfluous letter, why doesn't it simply state, "They camped at A, B, C, etc.?"

**Answer:** Rabbi Abraham Twerski explains that the forty years in the desert were a period of spiritual growth and development necessary to prepare the Jews for entrance into Israel. The people that were capable of the lack of faith and trust in Hashem manifested by the Golden Calf and the episode of the spies required a lengthy course in spiritual development, which they received under the tutelage of Moshe.

Each encampment symbolizes another step in this process of spiritual development. While achieving spirituality is essential, it must proceed gradually. Only after the Jews had solidified their spiritual growth at one particular encampment were they able to travel to the next point, and if they regressed in their spiritual development, they had to go back and recoup the spirituality they had lost before they were able to progress further.

**Lesson:** We have to remember that growth in life is a gradual process, one step at a time!

**Source:** Living Each Week (Rabbi Abraham Twerski)

## III. 2016

**Background:** The Torah gives clear instruction on how to make pots Kosher. It is imperative to remove any non-Kosher food that was absorbed in the vessel before using it for Kosher food. First, it is necessary to clean out the vessel very well and to remove any rust. Then the vessel must be Kashered in the same manner that it was previously used. For example, if it were used directly on the fire, it needs to have direct contact with fire to render it fit to be used. If non-Kosher food was cooked in it with boiling water, it now needs to be immersed in boiling water to remove what was absorbed.

**Question:** What lessons can we learn from making a pot Kosher?

**Answer:** The Chofetz Chaim commented that the same process applies to purifying people from their spiritual impurities and defects. First, a person must remove the "rust" of his transgressions by means of repentance. That means regretting what one has done wrong and accepting upon oneself not to continue doing those things in the future.

Afterward, one needs to be careful that the positive actions he does will replace the negative behavior on the same level. If one was enthusiastic and energetic in doing wrong, he should now have similar enthusiasm and energy when doing good. He should now use what he has erred with to make amends. For example, if one used his ability to speak to relate gossip and Loshon Harah, he should now utilize speech for fulfilling Mitzvos.

**Lesson:** When we make mistakes, we have to learn from them, remove the "rust," and make the improvements with the same enthusiasm that we originally made the mistake!

**Source:** Rabbi Pliskin in Growth Through Torah

# IV. 2017

**Background:** If a person killed another accidentally, he goes to the Arei Miklat until the Kohein Gadol dies. Then the person goes free.

**Question:** What does the Kohein Gadol have to do with this?

**Answer:** Since he was the leader of the generation, it was his job to daven daily that nothing bad would happen to the Jews. Since something bad happened, it shows that his davening wasn't perfect and the Kohein Gadol is partially responsible.

**Lesson:** We see how important Hashem considered the davening of a leader (Kohein Gadol). In some way, we are each leaders (e.g., of family, friends, etc.), and therefore, Hashem takes our davening seriously as well!

**Source:** Little Midrash Says, page 279

# V. 2018

**Background:**
- **First Part of Parsha:** Parshas Masai begins by telling over the travels of the Jews. The Torah lists the forty-two encampments that Klal Yisrael stopped at during their journey from Egypt into Eretz Yisrael. The Torah spends a considerable amount of pesukim telling us every stop, utilizing the formula, "They traveled from A and they encamped at B; and they traveled from B and encamped at C; and so forth." It catalogs 40 years and 42 stops of travels in the wilderness.
- **Second Part of Parsha:** Towards the end of Masai (chapter 35), the land of Canaan is divided up and each tribe is given a designated portion of land, except for one – the Leviim. Their portion of land was to be provided by all the other tribes. Hashem instructs Moshe that it was the responsibility of the entire Jewish people to provide the Leviim with cities and open space. The Leviim received 48 cites: 6 of them were Arei Miklat (cities of refuge for people who killed someone by accident) and the other 42 were regular Leviim cities.

**Question:** What is the significance of the numerical correspondence between the 42 camps/waypoints mentioned in the recounting of the years of wandering (Bamidbar 33) and the fact that 42 of the 48 Levite cities mentioned in the same Parsha (Masai) are of the ordinary non-refuge kind (Bamidbar 35:6)?

**Answer:** Rabbi Shlomo Kluger in his Sefer Imrei Shefer explains that the 42 cities that the Jewish People gave to the Leviim corresponded to the 42 journeys in the wilderness. At each resting spot in the desert, Hashem changed it from being desolate to a place of habitat. The Jewish people needed to repay this kindness to Hashem, and they did so by giving the Leviim (who were servants of Hashem) 42 cities in which to live; one city for every place they had traveled. The same way Hashem gave us a place to live in the desert, so too, He wanted us to give the Leviim a place to live, all in the interest of teaching us how to do Chesed.

**Lesson:** When a kindness is performed for us – whether it is by Hashem or anyone else – we should look for ways to "pay it forward" to other people.

## V. 2019

**Question:** Why does the Torah list out all 42 places that the Jewish people traveled? Why does the Torah need to be so specific in naming each location?

**Answer:** The Ramban (33:1) quotes the Rambam, who explains that while the miracles of the desert were well known to those who encountered them, future generations could be skeptical. In particular, while the Torah tells us that the Ma'an would fall every day, future generations might think that the Jewish people were close to surrounding cities, where food would have been provided to them. To ensure that future generations would not think this, the Torah documented the specific cities where they traveled, so people would know it was in the middle of the desert, away from any form of civilization. This documentation would ensure future generations believed and understood the miracles that took place.

**Our Observation #1:** It is fascinating to think that future generations could believe in the totality of the Torah, including the facts that Ma'an fell from Heaven every day, yet would be skeptical of it had the Torah not listed the specific cities!

**Our Observation #2:** When miracles are documented and written down, it creates a formality that is solidified for generations to come!

**Lesson:** Although the miracles today are not in the overt nature that the Jews experienced in the desert, we should document, in specific detail, any Chesed and miracles that Hashem performs for us, so that future generations will believe and appreciate the Chesed that Hashem did for us in our lifetime!

# Parshas Devarim

## I. 2014 (Song)

*(tune of "This is the song that never ends...")*

It's now the last book of Torah,
It's called Devarim with great laws.
Moshe re-caps significant events,
He speaks to all Jews once more, remember to repent.

Remind them all about the spies,
Speaking bad was not so wise.
We had to travel around Edom nation,
But others didn't let us, they were very bad men.

Remember how Hashem saved us,
From Sichon, Og, and other's fuss,
Now remember, any new bad king,
Hashem will save us yet again, from their bad tidings.

## II. 2017

**Question:** We know that the Jewish people are compared to the stars in the heavens. Moshe Rabbeinu told the Jewish people (1:10) "...behold, you are like the stars in the heavens in abundance (Lerov)." The obvious question is that there were much fewer Jews than stars! What did Moshe Rabbeinu mean?

**Answer:** The word Lerov, which has been translated as "abundance," can also mean greatness. The intention then of the verse is that even though when we look at the stars they seem tiny, this is in fact not true. In reality, they are gigantic. It is in this respect that the Jewish people are compared to the stars. Each Jew seems like a simple, small person. But the truth is that each Jew has massive potential. Hashem has imbued each one of us with the ability to change the world. Every Mitzvah we do brings Bracha to the world and Chas Ve'shalom, every transgression, brings destruction to the world. The world is in our hands.

**Lesson:** We need to remember that we have a very high potential and can accomplish great things!

**Source:** Baal Shem Tov, as quoted by Rabbi Michael Glass

# III. 2019

**Ramban Background:** The Ramban (see commentary to 1:18) explains the series of verses (1:15 – 1:18) where Moshe reminds the Jews of how the judicial system is arranged. Specifically, Moshe recounted his father-in-law Yisro's advice years earlier in the desert. Yisro recommended that Moshe teach the Jewish people Torah and Daven for them when they are in trouble. Additionally, advised Yisro, Moshe should appoint judges to help rule over various legal cases.

**Ramban Question:** If Moshe was reminding the Jews' of Yisro's advice in these verses, why didn't Moshe explicitly quote Yisro as the one who suggested these words of advice? After all, Pirkei Avos (6:6) tells us that when you credit the source, it helps bring the redemption! Why didn't Moshe quote Yisro?

**Ramban's Answer:** The Ramban offers three answers:

(1) Moshe did not want to mention Yisro's name because of humility. [There are various commentaries on the Ramban who differ as to whose humility this is referring. According to one opinion, it is Yisro since he was still traveling with the Jewish people. By quoting Yisro

in his presence, it would have embarrassed Yisro who was very humble and did not want the recognition. According to another opinion, it is Moshe's humility, since by mentioning Yisro's name, it would have appeared that Moshe was bragging about his father-in-law. See Artscroll's in-depth elucidation of the Ramban, page 30, Artscroll note 131.]

(2) Moshe did not want to mention Yisro's name because this would have called attention to the fact that Moshe married a woman from a non-Jewish nation many years earlier (even though she converted; it nonetheless would have brought up questions and discussions).

(3) It's plausible that Moshe consulted with Hashem on this matter and because it was Hashem's decision to put this judicial system in place, Moshe left out Yisro's name since this time it was Hashem's conclusion and did not pertain to Yisro at all.

**Our Observation:** According to the first and second explanations of the Ramban, bringing up Yisro's name would have triggered an emotional reaction. Whether it was an issue of humility/embarrassment (according to the first explanation) or drawing attention to the fact that Moshe had married a woman from a non-Jewish nation (according to the second explanation), the fact remains that Moshe was concerned he would elicit negative feelings and reactions. This is fascinating to comprehend, considering that the Jewish people intellectually already knew all of this information!

They were aware that Yisro had provided this advice years earlier. They were aware that Moshe had married a woman from a non-Jewish nation. The entire Jewish nation knew all of this information for years already! Yet, Moshe was concerned that the mere mentioning of Yisro's name would have triggered an emotional reaction, wreaking havoc, embarrassment, and unnecessary conversations.

**Lesson:** Sometimes we are around people who are aware of information, but the mere mention of a word or concept might generate an emotional reaction that is counterproductive or negative. We should do our best to be sensitive to people's feelings and not say anything that could create harmful emotional reactions!

# Parshas Va'eschanan

## I. 2014 (Song)
*(tune of "Tzur Mishelo...")*

Va'eschanan starts with a plea,
From Moshe, saying please let me.

Moshe begged Hashem with lots of davening,
Hashem said, "I'm sorry, you won't be going,"
Moshe was quite sad, but he didn't get mad,
He won't be going to Eretz Yisroel.

Now it's time to say the Ten Commandments.
It truly was a scene, amazing events.

Say the Shema Yisroel,
Cover your eyes real well,
It means Hashem is One,
We are the lucky sons.

Put on Tefillin each day,
Use them to Daven and pray,
Torah's inside of them,
A special precious gem.

Make sure to put Mezuzzah's on each door,
All through the house, and even at your store.

They are true protection,
Kiss them, do introspection,
Always remember that Hashem is our protector.
Home is where you sleep, learn Torah and eat,
Hashem is the boss, up and down the street.

## II. 2015

**Question:** Moshe pleads with Hashem to enter Israel. Why did Moshe want to go into Israel so badly?

**Answer:** There are many Mitzvos that can only be performed in Israel, and Moshe loved Hashem and the Torah so much that he wanted to be in Israel to do as many Mitzvos as he could.

**Lesson:** We should be like Moshe and look for as many opportunities as we can to do Mitzvos!

**Source:** Weekly Dvar by Rabbi Shlomo Ressler

## III. 2016

**Question:** When Moshe asked Hashem to go into Israel, he asked Hashem to give it to him as a gift. Why didn't he say he deserved it, based on all the Mitzvos he performed and the manner in which he led the Jewish People?

**Answer:** Moshe was teaching us the secret to how to ask Hashem for anything in our davening. We should always realize we don't deserve anything. Everything we ask for is a gift.

**Source:** In the Garden of the Torah (the Lubavitcher Rebbe, Rabbi Menachem M. Schneerson)

## IV. 2017

**Question:** What is the meaning of the word Mezuzah?

*Level 3 and Beyond!*

**Answer:** "Mezuzah" means "door-post." Also, the Hebrew word "Mezuzos" (plural) found in this Parsha, if rearranged, the letters can spell the two words, "Zaz Maves" which means "pushing away death." Thus, a Kosher Mezuzah acts as protection even to the extent of saving from death! In Tehillim, King David says, "Hashem shall protect your exit and your entry from now and forever." Our sages say that this applies to the Mezuzah.

**Lesson:** The Mezuzah acts as a shield and protects us, not only when we are inside the home but also when we go out.

**Source:** Torahfax on August 2, 2017

# V. 2018

**Question:** Moshe petitions to enter the land of Israel and was denied (3:26). Why didn't he at least merit having his bones buried in the land of Israel so that he could enter it posthumously, as did Yaakov and his 12 sons?

**Answer:** Rabbeinu Bechaye suggests that Hashem specifically wanted Moshe to be buried outside of the land of Israel for two reasons. First, this was done to show respect to the rest of the Jews in his generation who died in the wilderness and were buried there. Second, it gives hope to all Jews throughout the generations who lived outside of the land of Israel and who yearned for the ultimate redemption but didn't merit seeing it in their lifetimes. The recognition that Moshe himself died and was buried outside of Israel gives them encouragement that they will merit being resurrected and entering Israel together with him.

**Our Observation:** The common theme in both answers is that Hashem was concerned about the feelings of others. The ones who died in the desert (who deserved to be killed because they did Aveiros!) felt comforted that they were not alone. All those who would die in subsequent generations outside of Israel would be encouraged that, they too, one day will return to Israel with Moshe. In both answers, Hashem is being sensitive to the feelings of others – all at the expense of Moshe!

**Lesson:** We see how important it is to be considerate to other people's feelings, even where they may have been at fault, leading them to those consequences!

## VI. 2019

**Question:** This Parsha repeats the 10 Commandments, yet there are some differences between the first time they were cited (in Parshas Yisro) and in this Parsha. For example, when discussing the fourth commandment of keeping Shabbos, there seems to be conflicting reason as to why we are commanded to keep Shabbos. In Parshas Yisro (20:11), it says that Hashem commanded us to keep Shabbos to remember that Hashem created the entire world. In our Parsha, it seems to indicate (5:14) that Hashem commanded us to keep Shabbos so that we remember the events and miracles of leaving Egypt. Why is Hashem commanding us to keep Shabbos – to remember that He created the world or that He took us out of Egypt?

**Answer:** The Ramban (5:14) explains that ultimately, the whole point of Shabbos is to remember that Hashem created the world and controls everything. However, if there is ever a doubt in your mind that Shabbos testifies to His abilities, you should remember what your own eyes saw in Egypt – the amazing miracles that prove these very same concepts. As you start to think about the miracles that took place in Egypt (e.g., the ten plagues, splitting of the sea, etc.), you will realize that Hashem is the one who controls and creates all aspects of nature and everything in the world. Therefore, we should use the miracles from Egypt – which are tangible events that we saw first-hand – as a catalyst for getting to the ultimate message of Shabbos, which is the recognition that Hashem controls everything.

**Our Observation:** Based on this Ramban, had the Torah not instructed us to utilize the first-hand experiences of Mitzrayim as a trigger to recognize Hashem's control over the world, it is possible that a person could eventually doubt, God forbid, that Hashem created the world and controls everything! The tangible eye-witness accounts of the miracles in Egypt impact us because we experienced them first-hand. They confirm the critical message that Hashem is in charge of it all – which is the inherent message of Shabbos.

**Lesson:** Pay attention to first-hand experiences where Hashem shows you He is in charge. These real-world experiences can make a long-lasting impact!

# Parshas Eikev

## I. 2014 (Song)

*(to the tune of "Fiveish")*

Come to the world of Eikev,
Say hello to 7 fruits.
Wheat and barley,
Join us, follow suit.

Come to the land of Israel,
Hashem will give you every meal,
Just remember Hashem,
Is where it all stems from!

Ohhhh Hashem,
Thank you for our bread each day,
Ohhhh Hashem,
With the Golden Calf we strayed,
Ohhhh Hashem,
3 times we Daven and pray,
Ohhhh Hashem,
How can we ever repay?

## II. 2016

**Question:** In the Bircas HaMazon, it says, "And you shall eat and be satisfied and bless Hashem your G-d for the good land which He has given you." Why is it necessary to specifically mention the land during Benching?

**Answer:** Horav B.Z. Baruk, z'tl, explains with a Mashal: A person who was hungry and thirsty is walking in the desert with no food or water. Suddenly, a plane lands and a beautifully furnished home, complete with a table set with various delicacies, is ready for him! Obviously, in such a situation, his gratitude would extend beyond a simple acknowledgment of the delicious meal. He would appreciate everything, including the manner in which it was delivered. Similarly, we should acknowledge that every meal is a brand new creation, resulting from Hashem's benevolence and therefore, we don't just thank Hashem for the food, but also the land in which is originated!

**Lesson:** When we are thankful for something, we need to look at the whole picture and realize all the good that comes with it!

**Source:** Peninim on the Torah (Rabbi A.L. Scheinbaum)

# III. 2017

**Background:** The verse states (10:12), "…What does Hashem ask of you? Only to fear Hashem, to go in all His ways and to love Him, and to serve Hashem with all your heart and with all your soul." The Baal HaTurim explains that this verse is hinting at a statement from our Sages that we should say at least 100 Brachos every day. There are three allusions to this in the verse:

> (1) According to the "Aht Bash" letter exchange system [see explanation for what this system is in Artscroll's introduction to the in-depth elucidation of the Baal HaTurim], the letters "Mem" and "Heih" (from the word, "Mah") can be exchanged for the letters "Yud" and "Tzadei," which together are the numerical value of 100.
> (2) There are 100 Hebrew letters in the verse.
> (3) The Gematria of the word "Mimcha – You" is 100.
> Therefore, says the Baal HaTurim, this verse is an allusion to the Divrei Chazal that one should say 100 blessings every day.

**Our Observation:** Knowing that this verse is an allusion to saying 100 blessings every day, perhaps we can suggest that the literal reading of the verse is telling us *how* to say each one of those 100 Brachos. When the verse states "...What does Hashem ask of you?" and now we know it's the 100 Brachos that Hashem asks of us, the next part of the verse tells us *how* to make those blessings: through fear, love, with all your heart, and all your soul. As the verse continues: "....Only to *fear* Hashem, to go in all His ways and to *love* Him, and to serve Hashem with all your *heart* and with all your *soul*."

**Lesson:** We often say Brachos quickly and under our breath. If we took the time to explore the deepness and richness of the underlying words from each Bracha, we would actually realize there is great depth and wisdom to the words. Therefore, when we say a blessing, we should do it with fear, love, all your heart, and all your soul!

## IV. 2019

**Question:** The Torah tells us the positive commandment (8:10) that after you eat and are satisfied, you will thank Hashem for your food. What will make a person want to thank Hashem for giving them nourishment?

**Answer:** The Ramban explains that we will remember the difficult times we endured in Egypt and the affliction in the desert, which will allow us to truly appreciate all the good Hashem is doing for us now. We will thank Hashem as a result of realizing how good we have it, considering the tough times we had to endure.

**Our Observation:** The Ramban is teaching us we should use the tough times in our history as a catalyst to appreciate what we have now. It's fascinating that the reason we express our appreciation on food is more than just being satiated in eating – it is because we endured difficult times and should compare it to how fortunate we are now!

**Lesson:** If you ever encountered a challenging circumstance and endured it successfully (which we all have!), compare it to your current state and it will help you express gratitude and appreciation to Hashem!

# Parshas Re'eh

## I. 2014 (Song)

*(Tune of "Sofia the First" theme song)*

Re'eh begins by Moshe telling the Jews,
Idols in Canaan are very bad news.
If you want a Kosher animal,
Shechita in full you must do.

Hashem's prophet is special and called a Navi,
These are people just for royalty.
Three times a year go to the Beis Hamikdash,
I'm so excited with glee (*Yeshiva Comes First!*)

Tzedakah is what being royal's all about (*Yeshiva Comes First!*)
Help poor people each and every day (*Yeshiva*)

It's gonna be my time (*Yeshiva*)
To show them all that
*Yeshiva Comes First!*

## II. 2015

**Question:** In regards to Succos, the Torah refer to rejoicing twice. Why is there a second rejoicing only for Succos?

**Answer:** The second reference is a promise that someone who rejoices during Succos will merit to be joyful all year long. Succos has the power to spread its joyfulness during the entire year because Hashem makes us leave our homes and its protection in order to make us realize that everything in this world is transitory and that ultimately He protects us, not our material goods and fortresses.

**Lesson:** By realizing that it is only Hashem whom we can rely on, it will bring us peace and happiness throughout the year.

**Source:** Rabbi Dovid Feinstein

# III. 2019

**Background:** The Torah talks about the holiness of Israel and how idolatry has to be removed from the land. In these verses, the Torah says (12:5), "you shall seek out His Presence and come here." This is referencing that the Jews should take their sacrifices and bring them to Hashem's house (e.g., Beis Hamikdash / Mishkan).

**Ramban Explanation:** The Ramban explains that "seeking out Hashem" means that a person should travel from far distances to come to Hashem's house, and on the way there, the person should be asking the bystanders, "How do I get to Hashem's house?" and then encourage them to join by saying, "Come, let us go together to the mountain of Hashem!"

As the commentaries explain on this Ramban, even if you don't need any directions and you know how to get there, you should still actively engage in discussion with the people on the way, generate enthusiasm, and inspire them to come with you. (See Yalkut Shemoni as quoted by the footnote in Artscroll's in-depth elucidation of the Ramban, page 286, footnote 13).

**Our Observation:** It is fascinating to note that the Ramban's suggestion for generating excitement and encouraging bystanders is initiated by simply asking for directions and engaging in basic conversation. There is no lucrative incentive, dramatic plea, or even logical debate as to why they should come. It seems that the mere engagement in simple conversation can be enough to ignite interest, excitement, and even enthusiasm in coming to Hashem's holy place.

Perhaps we can suggest that the reason for this is because every person has a special Neshama (e.g., a soul that is a piece of Hashem in them), and when it comes to the holiness of Hashem's Torah and/or presence in the Mishkan, a person is naturally drawn to such a mission. All it takes is a simple conversation or discussion to ignite that spark.

**Lesson:** When you are talking to people, you can encourage them to learn Torah or do Mitzvos through simple and basic conversation. Just ask about their welfare, invite them to join you for a Mitzvah, and you will likely unlock a spark of excitement within them!

# Parshas Shoftim

## I. 2014 (Song)

*(tune of "Yo Ho Matey's Away")*

Shoftim's about a King,
Torah's a treasure and adventure today,
Let's Go!
3 Special Mitzvos, don't be a Chazer,
Together as a team
King and the Torah land guidance,
And me!

When a soldier goes to war,
Hashem helps him be safe even more,
Let's go!
Sometimes, soldiers go,
Back to their home,
King and the Torah land guidance
And me!

We learn about Baal Tashchis,
Don't waste or you'll be remissed,
Let's go!
Food, paper, and many other things,
Together as a team,
King and the Torah land guidance
And me!

## II. 2016

**Question:** The Torah tells us that as the Jews are preparing for war, there are four types of people who are exempt from fighting and are allowed to go home. They are: (1) a person who built a new home, but has not yet lived in it; (2) a person who has planted a vineyard, but has not yet eaten from the produce; (3) a person who is engaged, but has not yet gotten married; and (4) a person who is scared. While we can easily understand the rationale for why the fourth group of people went home (e.g., people afraid of fighting), why did the Torah make the other three groups exempt from fighting?

**Answer #1:** In the first three groups, those people would have their minds on other things (e.g., their house, new fruits, or fiancé) and would, therefore, be distracted from fighting. Therefore, Hashem exempted them from war.

**Answer #2:** The Torah didn't want to embarrass a person who said they were afraid to go to war. Therefore, Hashem provided three other groups – a person not yet living in their new house, not yet eating from their vineyard, and not yet married – so that when a person was dismissed from going to war, the true reason wasn't readily known to the entire group. According to this answer, the first three groups, were in actuality, a decoy for the person who was afraid of war. This is the extent to which the Torah ensures a person should not be embarrassed.

**Lesson:** According to the second answer, we learn how far we must go to prevent the embarrassment of another person!

**Source:** Little Midrash Says, pages 158 – 162

# III. 2019

**Background:** The Torah commands us that we must appoint a Jewish King over our nation. One of the laws about the King is that (17:16), "…he shall not have too many horses for himself, so that he shall not return the people to Egypt in order to increase horses, for

Hashem has said to you, 'You shall no longer return on this road again.'" The Ramban explains that the verse is telling us two separate stipulations for the King:

(1) The King should not have too many horses for himself. As the Ramban explains, this is because it could, G-d forbid, lead him to put more trust into his mighty army/horses instead of Hashem.

(2) The King should not send purchasing representatives to live in Egypt. In those days, it was common that selling horses and other animals was a big investment and manner in which to make money. In order to export and sell horses from Egypt, you needed to have connections with the Pharaoh and essentially, live in Egypt. This would allow representatives from other nations to buy horses from Egypt and ship them to where they needed to go, helping their nation with economic gain. According to the Ramban, this command is that the Jewish King should not send Jewish purchasing agents to live in Egypt.

The Ramban explains the reason for this is because the Egyptians were exceptionally wicked and Hashem does not want the Jewish people to learn from their evil ways. Hashem says we should never live in Egypt ever again.

**Our Question:** The second stipulation for the King – that he cannot ever send purchasing representatives to live in Egypt – is a law that applies for all time. This was not a limited-time restriction, but rather one that is contingent forever. Isn't that a bit harsh, considering that the Egyptians who sinned against Hashem during the times of the Jews' slavery eventually died? It was now an entirely new generation and group of people – why would Hashem continue to impose this restriction for eternity? Furthermore, wouldn't the Jewish purchasing representatives isolate themselves and stay away from the Egyptians? These Jews would presumably know the deep Egyptian history and keep far away from these Egyptians whose ancestors were exceedingly wicked to their Jewish ancestors. Would such a living arrangement impact them that greatly?

**Our Suggested Answer:** It's possible to suggest that once exceedingly wicked sins are committed against Hashem, the stain and blemish is ingrained in that society and culture for eternity. Generations and people can come and go, but the residual effect of what transpired in Egypt will always be reminiscent. This extends to such a degree that even generations later, the residual impact of negative behavior lingers. Therefore, even if the Jewish purchasing representatives attempted to remain isolated from the Egyptians, they would be unable to completely do so, since the negative residue and behavior would forever be etched into the fabric of Egyptian society and people.

**Lesson:** Be careful with whom and where you surround yourself! They have a big impact on you!

# Parshas Ki Tetzei

## I. 2014 (Song)

*(tune of Disney's "Hot Dog, Hot Dog, Hot Diggity Dog")*

Ki Tetzei says to marry a Jew
Return lost objects to their crew,
Be sensitive and chase the mother bird,
Remember Miriam, speak good words.

Put a fence around a porch or roof,
Your ox and donkey, don't be aloof
Tell the truth in business, it's the law,
Don't cheat or steal, not even a straw.

Amalek are very very bad guys,
They tried to attack us by surprise.

The lesson we learn from picking your spouse (*That's me!*),
They'll create your house!

## II. 2015

**Question:** The Torah tells us that you can not have a donkey and ox pull a wagon together. You can have 2 oxen or 2 donkeys, but not one of each together. Why?

**Answer:** The Daas Zekeinim explains that since an ox chews its cud and a donkey doesn't, the donkey will be envious when it sees that the ox has food in his mouth, and he doesn't. Even though they may have both received the same ration of food, the perception of the donkey is that the ox has more since he chews longer. Rabbi Chaim

Shmuelevitz commented that this is a great lesson in how careful we must be not to cause others the pain of envy.

**Lesson:** If we must be careful with the feelings of an animal, all the more so must we be careful with the feelings of another person. Be careful not to boast about your accomplishments or possessions if others might feel envious.

**Source:** Growth Through Torah by Rabbi Zelig Pliskin

# III. 2017

**Background:** Hashem reminds us how important it is to be perfectly honest: "a perfect and honest weight...and measure you shall have." Not only shouldn't a merchant cheat by selling something on a bad scale, he shouldn't even own one.

**Question:** Why is it a problem to own a bad scale if you will never use it?

**Answer:** Hashem doesn't want a person to even be tempted to use it. Honesty is so important to Hashem that you can't even own a bad scale in your house. The Torah teaches us that behaving honestly is one of the most crucial ways to improve society and to improve ourselves.

**Lesson:** Make sure to always tell the truth!

**Source:** http://www.aish.com/tp/pak/fp/48884442.html

# IV. 2018

**Question:** What is one of the worst traits of Amalek?

*Level 3 and Beyond!*

**Answer:** In the posuk (Devarim 25:18), it says the word "Korcha" in reference to Amalek, stating, "That he happened upon you on the way." The Rashbam explains the word Korcha (happened) is connected to the word "Mikreh – coincidence." Amalek believes that everything is a coincidence and nothing is controlled by Hashem. Jewish people believe the opposite – that everything is Hashgacha Pratis and controlled by Hashem!

**Lesson:** It's so important to remember that Hashem is in control of everything and each and every detail is Hashgacha Pratis!

**Source:** Rashbam, as quoted by Aleinu L'Shabeach (page 317)

# Parshas Ki Savo

## I. 2013 (Song)

*(tune of "Yankee Doodle")*

This week's Parsha is called Ki Savo,
And it's about Bikkurim,
Which means bringing the first fruits to the Kohein with a "thank you" theme.

We learn to be like Hashem, our G-d, with Mercy and with Chesed,
That means being kind to everyone, and it is highly recommended.

Moshe told the Jewish People when they get to Israel,
They would write the Torah on 12 stones to show that it was real.

Moshe wrote it in 70 languages,
So they would all understand it.

And the people learned that if they followed it they would get rewarded!

The lesson of the Parsha is to say, "Hashem, THANK YOU"
Because that's really what it means to be a Jew!

## II. 2015

**Question:** Moshe tells his people that when they enter Israel, they are to take "the first of the fruits" and bring it to "the place that G-d will choose." This is the commandment of Bikkurim, the ceremonious bringing of the new fruits to Jerusalem. Why doesn't the Torah tell us how much to bring?

**Answer:** It is interesting to note that while the law of Bikkurim stressed that the very first fruits to ripen be consecrated, there was no minimum quantity required. One grape or one fig could technically fulfill the letter of the law. This teaches us that Hashem is interested not in the quantity of fruits, but that it's your first fruit, showing your true priority.

**Lesson:** We need to determine what is the Ikar (main priority) and what is the Taful (secondary). If we do the important things first, Hashem will know what our priorities are.

**Source:** Reflections on the Sedra by Rabbi Zalman Posner

# III. 2016

**Background:** Baal HaTurim states that the word "Teneh" (basket) has the Gematria of 60, which is an allusion to the Midrash which states that a person should bring 1/60 of their fruits as the Bikkurim. The Baal HaTurim continues and states that the only Hebrew letter not in the entire chapter of Bikkurim is the Hebrew letter "Samech," which has the Gematria of 60 as well.

**Question:** If the Samech is 60, and is an allusion to the 1/60 a person is supposed to bring, why is that letter absent from the chapter on Bikkurim? Shouldn't it be included?

**Answer:** The whole message of the Bikkurim is that Hashem is in charge and runs the world. Hashem is the One who provides you with food, and hence, the first fruits go to Hashem. The Samech is round – like the basket the Bikkurim are brought in – and the shape of the Samech is indicative of a person going around and around in "circles" without ever stopping to see Hashem in their lives. They get up, go to work, come home, go to sleep, and do it all over again; often not stopping to "see" Hashem in their lives. The Samech is missing from the Bikkurim chapter to show us that we often don't "see" Hashem if we are not looking for Him. But when we do look for Him, we will find Him, and be able to learn the lesson of the Bikkurim!

**Lesson:** Everything in our lives comes from Hashem and we have to make an active effort to see Him in our lives.

**Source:** Rabbi Shalom Rosner on the Parsha 5776:
https://www.ou.org/torah/parsha/rabbi-rosner-on-parsha/ki-tavo-5776-2/
See source sheet: https://www.ou.org/torah/files/ki_savo_5776.pdf

# IV. 2017

**Background:** When a farmer brings the Bikkurim, he has to make a speech. In this speech, he talks about the historical background and then talks about how the Jews inherited Israel and how the Jews are now able to bring their crops as Bikkurim. In the historical background section of the speech, the farmer talks about how an Armenian (this was referring to Lavan) tried to destroy Yaakov.

**Question:** Why does that speech start talking about Yaakov and Lavan? This seems like it's in the middle of the story – why skip over Avraham and Yitzchak? What is the relevance of Yaakov/Lavan to the Bikkurim?

**Answer:** Of all the Avos, Yaakov is the one who knew what it meant to be homeless. Avraham lived in Israel most of his life (after Hashem told him to go there) and Yitzchak lived in Israel his entire life. Yaakov, on the other hand, was chased away from his home at a young age by Eisav, he then spent 20 years working for Lavan, and then, when he was finally able to settle down in Israel, he was brought to Egypt because of Yosef and lived there for the rest of his life.

Yaakov was displaced his whole life. Only someone who is missing something can be truly appreciative when they receive it. So, when the farmer makes the speech about receiving Israel as an inheritance – the home of the Jewish people – it is only appropriate to reference the only one who felt more displaced than anyone else – Yaakov. Because when a person truly feels they are lacking something – and then they get it – they appreciate it on an entirely new level.

**Lesson:** The secret to sincere appreciation is the ability to live your life as if everything was taken away from you, and then you got it back.

**Source:** Rabbi Frand "The Power of a Vort," pages 311-312 and 316-317

# V. 2018

**Background:** The Bikkurim ceremony was one of the most exciting and jubilant events that occurred. As each farmer would take their first fruits to Yerushalayim, there was a processional that included music, dancing, singing, and an incredibly joyous tone. The Torah says (26:11), "Ve'Samachta Bechol HaTov – You should rejoice in all the good that Hashem has given you…"

**Question:** If this was an environment of excitement and happiness, why is there an explicit command in the Torah to "rejoice in all the good?" Shouldn't it be self-evident and expected that the farmer will be naturally happy because of the surrounding festivities? Why would the Torah seemingly use those words for no reason?

**Answer:** Rav Gifter explains that a person can be in the most exciting and happy environment, yet that unto itself does not guarantee happiness. This could happen when a person is jealous of another or is simply greedy. The farmer may look to his right and see another farmer who has even more delicious apples than he does; perhaps they are more colorful or appealing. Further, perhaps the farmer wishes he could have brought more fruits as a result of him having more fruit trees. If the farmer were to have these feelings, despite his festive surroundings, he would still remain unhappy! Therefore, the Torah instructs the farmer to "rejoice in all the good that Hashem gave you" so that the farmer takes a moment to appreciate what Hashem gave him, and not compare his situation to anyone else.

**Lesson:** You can be in the happiest place on earth, surrounded by the best circumstances, but if you don't adjust your attitude, you will never be happy! When we ensure our attitudes are proper, we will be happy no matter what circumstances we find ourselves in!

**Source:** Rabbi Wiesenfeld quoting Rav Gifter on this shiur: https://torahanytime.com/#/lectures?v=66431

# VI. 2019

**Background:** In the beginning of Parshas Ki Savo, the posuk tells us that the first fruits are dedicated to Hashem. This is referring to the Bikkurim. The Baal HaTurim explains (26:2) that the first of everything is dedicated to Hashem. This includes (1) the first grains (which become Terumah); (2) our very first conquest of the city of Yericho, which was set aside as segregated property to Hashem; and (3) the first words a child speaks should also be ones of Torah (e.g., the father should teach the child the phrase "Torah Tzivah Lanu Moshe…" and also the first line of Shema).

**Question:** In reference to dedicating the "first" of something to Hashem, it is understandable to do so with inanimate objects – such as fruit, grain, or cities. However, in regard to the Baal HaTurim's last example – designating the child's first words to be ones of Torah – how can we consider this a dedication of the child, given that the child might later change their mind and, Heaven forbid, reject the Torah?

**Our Suggested Answer:** Perhaps we can suggest that making the effort and laying the foundation that the child's first words are Torah articulate the direction in which the child is set. Although the child has free will and can choose their own direction later in life, the fact will forever remain that their first words – the foundation of their existence – was dedicated to living a Torah lifestyle. Although the child is young and does not understand all the implications at that time, the impact it makes on their life is long-lasting, as nobody will ever be able to ever take away their first words and the path that their parents made for them. More than anything else, it proves that the parents' mind is directed and thinking about Hashem since the first words they want their child to say are ones of Torah.

**Lesson:** Never underestimate the power of "first" impressions or dedications. When embarking on anything in life – a big project, trip, raising a child, or even a simple conversation – use the opportunity to set the initial direction in the path of Torah – because that shows where your mind is directed!

# Parshas Netzavim

## I. 2013 (Song)

*(tune of "Hi-Ho, Hi Ho, it's off to work we go..." from Seven Dwarfs)*

Netzavim-Vayeilech, it's a double Parsha,
It's about doing Mitzvos and learning Torah.

Moshe wrote, a Torah for the tribe of Levi,
And all the tribes wanted one too, so Moshe wrote many.

Hakhel, is a special Mitzvah on Succos,
In the Beis Hamikdash, the king reads to us.

It's a Mitzvah to write your own Torah,
And if you can't, buy Torah books and Gemara!

The lesson of the Parsha is to be a Torah Jew,
Because we know Hashem loves all of us, too!

## II. 2015

**Question:** "You are standing this day, all of you, before G-d...to enter the covenant which G-d makes with you this day...that He may establish you this day unto Himself." Three times Moshe stresses "this day" – why?

**Answer:** There are two natural roadblocks placed before us as we endeavor to become better people and better Jews, and both of these roadblocks can be overcome by focusing on "this day." The first natural roadblock is our inclination to look ahead at temptations and hurdles we will encounter. We often feel frustration and helplessness in overcoming those collective obstacles. The Torah therapeutically empowers us to focus on one day at a time, and leave tomorrow's worries for another day. The second natural roadblock we face is the guilt of our past, which can sometimes make us feel depressed and unworthy. We have today to repent for those things we shouldn't have done. The time is right now, and "this day" is just right.

In his final words to the Jews, Moshe urges them to follow the commandments of the Torah, telling them that they will be rewarded for doing so (and conversely punished if they deviate). However, there are moments of temptation when even the promise of reward or threat of punishment are insufficient to control one's behavior. Moshe teaches us that the key to success is "this day" – adapting to a lifestyle of taking it one day at a time.

**Lesson:** By concentrating only on today and avoiding worrying about the future or the past, we will follow the Torah's commandments without the stress!

**Source:** Living Each Week by Rabbi Avraham Twerski

# III. 2016

**Background:** Moshe Rabbeinu spoke to the Jewish people. He stressed that all of the Jewish people were there, from the leaders all the way down to the woodchoppers and water drawers (29:9-10).

**Question:** Why were the woodchoppers and water drawers singled out?

**Answer:** Consider the following Mashal (parable): A diamond dealer once met Rav Shalom Dov Ber Schneerson at a diamond fair. The dealer asked him why he devoted so much time to simple Jews. Rav Shalom inquired of the diamond dealer if he had brought any diamonds to the fair. The dealer replied that he had. Rav Shalom then asked if he could see them. The dealer took out a bag, opened it up, and pointed out one that was very special. Rav Shalom looked at it and exclaimed that he could not see anything special about it. The merchant responded that to appreciate a diamond you need to be a diamond expert. At that point, Rav Shalom told him that the same is true with a simple Jew. You have to be an expert to appreciate their qualities. The Nimshal is that every Jew has special qualities, and although sometimes they are covered up and hard to see, they are nonetheless there and can be made to shine.

**Lesson:** Hashem wants us to realize that we are each special to Him and each has a unique mission to achieve.

**Source:** Pachad Dovid

# IV. 2018

**Question:** What is the significance of the number of Pesukim in this Parsha and the remaining Parshios for the rest of the year?

**Answer:** Rav Moshe Wolfson notices that Parshas Netzavim is 40 pesukim, Vayeilech 30, and Haazinu 52. He says these 3 represent the different types of Jews, and when they receive their verdict for the new year.

There are those who begin their repentance on Rosh Chodesh Elul, and for 30 days they do Teshuva. These are the Tzadikim, and on Rosh Hashana, they are immediately inscribed in the Book of Life.

Then there are those who have to wait 40 days, the Beinonim. Their lives hang in the balance. Hopefully, they do Teshuva, and on Yom Kippur, after 40 days, they are inscribed in the Book of Life.

And then, of course, there are those who are not inspired and don't wake up; not for Rosh Hashana and not for Yom Kippur. They have to wait until the very last moment, Hoshana Rabbah, when the final judgment is brought; after 52 days.

But ultimately, no matter when it is, we receive our judgment, "V'zos HaBracha."

**Lesson:** Hopefully, we become righteous enough to be able to be inscribed on Rosh Hashana. If not, we must do Teshuva and hopefully Yom Kippur. But ultimately, no matter when it is, as long as we do Teshuva; up until the very last moment, Hashem is there and waiting, ready and eager to inscribe us in the Book of Life and for a year of blessing.

**Source:** Inspiration Daily by Rabbi Spero on September 5, 2018

# Parshas Vayeilech

## I. 2015

**Question:** The Mitzvah of Hakhel required everyone to come. All women, men, and children. Why did the babies have to come? Wouldn't they disturb the other people? Plus, they wouldn't remember it anyway! Why should they come?

**Answer:** That's how powerful and important the Torah is – even on children, it will impact them for the rest of their lives, and it's worth the sacrifice!

## II. 2016

**Question:** The Mitzvah of Hakhel's stated purpose is to imbue the younger generation with the fear of G-d and the commitment to observe the Torah. It is scheduled on the Succos that immediately follows the Shemittah year (i.e., the seventh year during which the land is to lie fallow). The celebration of this Mitzvah is when the king of Israel stood upon a specially designed stage and read the Book of Devarim. Why did it have to follow the Shemittah year? Wouldn't it have been equally impressive at any time?

**Answer:** Allowing the land to lie fallow was both a personal sacrifice and a test of faith. Israel was primarily an agricultural country, and this Mitzvah was an act of Mesiras Nefesh (placing oneself at great risk). What the Torah is telling us is that if we wish our children and grandchildren to adopt the values we espouse, we must demonstrate to them the depth and sincerity of our convictions. That's why the Mitzvah of Hakhel comes right after Shemittah – so the children can see just how important the Torah is to their parents – they actually live it through faith. This is what the children just saw first-hand during the Shemittah year!

**Lesson:** Mesiras Nefesh doesn't necessarily require heroic acts. Indeed, it may more often be manifested in less dramatic behavior, such as committing oneself to davening, learning, giving Tzedakah, and other daily Mitzvos.

**Source:** Rabbi Twerski

## III. 2017

**Background:** Immediately after the Shemittah year, on Succos, the Torah tells us about the Mitzvah of Hakhel – where the entire Jewish people would gather in the courtyard of the Beis Hamikdash to hear the king read from a select portion of the Torah. Everyone is required to go – men, women, and children. The Gemara in Chagigah (3a) explains that the reason for bringing small children to Hakhel is because Hashem wanted to give a reward to the people who bring them (e.g., the parents).

**Question #1:** The children don't understand the words being read by the King. Why is the Torah giving a reward for a useless act?

**Question #2:** Further, what reward is the Torah referring to that the parents will receive?

**Answer:** The Imrei Emes and Sifsei Tzadik explain that in reality, the small children will benefit from the sight of just being there with a large assembly, realizing the importance of the Torah. They will be inspired by seeing how much the entire nation treasures the Torah, and it will affect them so greatly that when they get old enough to learn it on their own, they will be excited to learn it themselves. The Torah, therefore, gives a special reward for merely exposing the children to such a sight. As the Mefarshim explain, the "reward" that the Gemara is referring to is a parent's ultimate Nachas – the satisfaction of seeing their children grow up to live a Torah lifestyle, which will occur based on the exposure to Hakhel the parents gave them when they were young.

**Lesson:** When children see adults who are excited to learn Torah, they will assume those same feelings as they get older!

**Source:** A Daily Dose of Torah (Series One), page 166 of Parshas Vayeilech

# Parshas Haazinu

## I. 2013 (Song)

*(Tune of: "Oh my darling, Oh my darling, Oh my darling, Clementine...")*

This week's Parsha is Haazinu, and it's a song that Moshe knew.
It compares Torah to raindrops, the source of all life – this is true.

If you have lots of Mazal, don't think it's all because of you,
Please remember that Hashem was the one who gave it to you.

Hashem told Moshe, "Go to Har Nebo, to see the holy land of Israel,
It will make you feel special and you'll even say, 'for real!'"

The lesson we learn from the Parsha is to know that Hashem is just,
And even when we don't understand it, this mentality is a must.

## II. 2015

**Background:** In the beginning of the song of Haazinu, Moshe asks the heaven and earth to be the witnesses to what he is telling the Jews (that if they do good things, they get rewarded, but if not, they get punished.)

**Question:** Why did Moshe have the heaven and earth be witnesses? Why not birds or trees or anything else?

**Answer:** The heavens and earth hold the keys to our food – if you keep the Mitzvos, the heavens will make rain fall and the earth will allow fruits, vegetables, and grain to grow. But if you don't keep the Torah, the heaven will hold back the rain and the earth will not produce food.

**Lesson:** Remember that Hashem controls all of nature.

**Source:** Little Midrash Says, page 271

# III. 2016

**Question:** In this Parsha, when Moshe is about to teach the Jewish People the song, the Torah says, "And Moshe came and spoke all the words of this song in the ears of the people, he, and Hoshea the son of Nun (32:44)." Many years earlier Moshe had changed the name of Hoshea to Yehoshua (Bamidbar 13:16). Why is he now reverting back to calling him "Hoshea?"

**Answer:** The Targum Yonatan ben Uziel (Bamidbar 13:16) writes that when Moshe observed the humbleness of Hoshea, he added a "Yud" to his name, which is the smallest letter of the Alef-Beis, and thus a symbol of humbleness, calling him Yehoshua.

This posuk discusses the Shabbos when the authority was taken from Moshe and given to Yehoshua. Now that Yehoshua was becoming the new leader of Klal Yisrael, his Rebbe, Moshe, referred to him as Hoshea, omitting the Yud. This was Moshe's way of telling him, "As the leader of the Jewish community, it is necessary that you be highly respected and feared by all. No longer may you humble yourself before all as you did until now" (see Kesubos 103b).

**Lesson:** You always need to be humble, but when you are in charge of a situation, you need to step up to the plate and ensure you are respected.

**Source:** Sichos on the Torah, see http://www.sie.org/templates/sie/article_cdo/aid/2865712/jewish/Questions-and-Answers-on-Haazinu.htm

*Level 3 and Beyond!*

# Parshas V'zos HaBracha

## I. 2016

**Background:** In Parshas V'zos HaBracha, the Torah attests to the fact that "There has never arisen a prophet like Moshe (34:1)." The Rambam adds that nobody has, or will ever raise themselves to that level, but everyone can be like Moshe.

**Question:** Rav Wasserman asks, however, that if the Torah says that no one will ever reach Moshe's level, how can the Rambam claim that anyone can?

**Answer:** The Lekach Tov answers that everyone has to accomplish what they can in life using the talents, abilities, and strengths they were given. In Moshe's case, he was given strength and wisdom beyond all others, and he used those to the maximum of his potential. It's only the combination of Moshe's innate gifts, combined with his utilization of those gifts to their full potential that made Moshe the best prophet the world has ever seen.

Although Moshe's combination of strength and wisdom will never be duplicated, the ability to use our talents and strengths is within each of us. The Rambam is telling us that although we'll never have all of Moshe's inherent capabilities, the potential to be as great is within us.

**Lesson:** We have to use our own talents and skills to accomplish our true potential and in that way, we can rise to the greatness of Moshe in our own ways.

**Source:** Weekly Dvar by Rabbi Shlomo Ressler

## II. 2019

**Question:** In Moshe's final moments of the Torah, we are told (34:1) that Hashem showed Moshe the entire land of Israel. Since Moshe was not allowed to go into Israel at all, why did Hashem go to such great lengths to show him the land in its entirety?

**Answer:** The Ramban explains (34:1) that the reason Hashem showed it to Moshe was because the land "was filled good things; the most desirous of all of the lands" and Hashem knew how happy Moshe would be for the Jewish people that they would get this benefit and enjoy it, so Hashem wanted Moshe to see it with his own two eyes.

**Our Observation:** Knowing how much Moshe wanted to go into Israel – this was the culmination of leaving Egypt and traveling through the desert for 40 years – one would think that Moshe would have felt just a tinge of disappointment by viewing the land he so wanted to enter. Moshe pleaded and begged Hashem (see Parshas Va'eschanan) hundreds of times to go into Israel, but Hashem ultimately denied his request. Certainly, Hashem would be sensitive to Moshe's feelings and not do anything to add "insult to injury" if Moshe were distraught. Rather, it must be that Hashem knew that Moshe's happiness for the people would outweigh his own personal disappointment. Hashem, therefore, shows Moshe the land, knowing he would be happy for the Jewish nation. This shows Moshe's deep-rooted connection to the Jewish people and how he was able to put his own feelings aside.

**Lesson:** Be happy for other people's successes, even when it might be personally difficult for you. Doing so will show how deep and close your relationship is with that person!

אוֹתָם וְאֶת בֵּיתָם וְאֶת זַרְעָם וְאֶת כָּל אֲשֶׁר לָהֶם אוֹתָנוּ וְאֶת כָּל אֲשֶׁר לָנוּ כְּמוֹ שֶׁנִּתְבָּרְכוּ אֲבוֹתֵינוּ אַבְרָהָם יִצְחָק וְיַעֲקֹב בַּכֹּל מִכֹּל כֹּל – כֵּן יְבָרֵךְ אוֹתָנוּ כֻּלָּנוּ יַחַד בִּבְרָכָה שְׁלֵמָה. וְנֹאמַר: אָמֵן.

בַּמָּרוֹם יְלַמְּדוּ עֲלֵיהֶם וְעָלֵינוּ זְכוּת שֶׁתְּהֵא לְמִשְׁמֶרֶת שָׁלוֹם. וְנִשָּׂא בְרָכָה מֵאֵת יְיָ וּצְדָקָה מֵאֱלֹהֵי יִשְׁעֵנוּ וְנִמְצָא חֵן וְשֵׂכֶל טוֹב בְּעֵינֵי אֱלֹהִים וְאָדָם.

בשבת: הָרַחֲמָן הוּא יַנְחִילֵנוּ יוֹם שֶׁכֻּלּוֹ שַׁבָּת וּמְנוּחָה לְחַיֵּי הָעוֹלָמִים.
ביום טוב: הָרַחֲמָן הוּא יַנְחִילֵנוּ יוֹם שֶׁכֻּלּוֹ טוֹב.
בראש חודש: הָרַחֲמָן הוּא יְחַדֵּשׁ עָלֵינוּ אֶת הַחֹדֶשׁ הַזֶּה לְטוֹבָה וְלִבְרָכָה.
בראש השנה: הָרַחֲמָן הוּא יְחַדֵּשׁ עָלֵינוּ אֶת הַשָּׁנָה הַזֹּאת לְטוֹבָה וְלִבְרָכָה.
בסוכות: הָרַחֲמָן הוּא יָקִים לָנוּ אֶת סֻכַּת דָּוִד הַנּוֹפָלֶת.

הָרַחֲמָן הוּא יְזַכֵּנוּ לִימוֹת הַמָּשִׁיחַ וּלְחַיֵּי הָעוֹלָם הַבָּא. מַגְדִּיל (מִגְדּוֹל) יְשׁוּעוֹת מַלְכּוֹ וְעֹשֶׂה חֶסֶד לִמְשִׁיחוֹ לְדָוִד וּלְזַרְעוֹ עַד עוֹלָם. עֹשֶׂה שָׁלוֹם בִּמְרוֹמָיו הוּא יַעֲשֶׂה שָׁלוֹם עָלֵינוּ וְעַל כָּל יִשְׂרָאֵל. וְאִמְרוּ: אָמֵן.

יְראוּ אֶת יְיָ קְדֹשָׁיו כִּי אֵין מַחְסוֹר לִירֵאָיו. כְּפִירִים רָשׁוּ וְרָעֵבוּ וְדֹרְשֵׁי יְיָ לֹא יַחְסְרוּ כָל טוֹב. הוֹדוּ לַיְיָ כִּי טוֹב כִּי לְעוֹלָם חַסְדּוֹ. פּוֹתֵחַ אֶת יָדֶךָ וּמַשְׂבִּיעַ לְכָל חַי רָצוֹן. בָּרוּךְ הַגֶּבֶר אֲשֶׁר יִבְטַח בַּיְיָ וְהָיָה יְיָ מִבְטַחוֹ. נַעַר הָיִיתִי גַּם זָקַנְתִּי וְלֹא רָאִיתִי צַדִּיק נֶעֱזָב וְזַרְעוֹ מְבַקֶּשׁ לָחֶם. יְיָ עֹז לְעַמּוֹ יִתֵּן יְיָ יְבָרֵךְ אֶת עַמּוֹ בַשָּׁלוֹם.

הָרַחֲמָן הוּא יִמְלוֹךְ עָלֵינוּ לְעוֹלָם וָעֶד. הָרַחֲמָן הוּא יִתְבָּרַךְ בַּשָּׁמַיִם וּבָאָרֶץ. הָרַחֲמָן הוּא יִשְׁתַּבַּח לְדוֹר דּוֹרִים וְיִתְפָּאַר בָּנוּ לָעַד וּלְנֵצַח נְצָחִים וְיִתְהַדַּר בָּנוּ לָעַד וּלְעוֹלְמֵי עוֹלָמִים.

הָרַחֲמָן הוּא יְפַרְנְסֵנוּ בְּכָבוֹד. הָרַחֲמָן הוּא יִשְׁבּוֹר עֻלֵּנוּ מֵעַל צַוָּארֵנוּ וְהוּא יוֹלִיכֵנוּ קוֹמְמִיּוּת לְאַרְצֵנוּ. הָרַחֲמָן הוּא יִשְׁלַח לָנוּ בְּרָכָה מְרֻבָּה בַּבַּיִת הַזֶּה וְעַל שֻׁלְחָן זֶה שֶׁאָכַלְנוּ עָלָיו. הָרַחֲמָן הוּא יִשְׁלַח לָנוּ אֶת אֵלִיָּהוּ הַנָּבִיא זָכוּר לַטּוֹב וִיבַשֵּׂר לָנוּ בְּשׂוֹרוֹת טוֹבוֹת יְשׁוּעוֹת וְנֶחָמוֹת.

בבית אביו אומר: הָרַחֲמָן הוּא יְבָרֵךְ אֶת אָבִי מוֹרִי בַּעַל הַבַּיִת הַזֶּה וְאֶת אִמִּי מוֹרָתִי בַּעֲלַת הַבַּיִת הַזֶּה.
נשוי אומר: הָרַחֲמָן הוּא יְבָרֵךְ אוֹתִי (אם אביו ואמו בחיים: וְאֶת אָבִי מוֹרִי, וְאֶת אִמִּי מוֹרָתִי) וְאֶת אִשְׁתִּי וְאֶת זַרְעִי וְאֶת כָּל אֲשֶׁר לִי.
נשואה אומרת: הָרַחֲמָן הוּא יְבָרֵךְ אוֹתִי (אם אביה ואמה בחיים: וְאֶת אָבִי מוֹרִי וְאֶת אִמִּי מוֹרָתִי) וְאֶת בַּעֲלִי וְאֶת זַרְעִי וְאֶת כָּל אֲשֶׁר לִי.
אורח אומר: הָרַחֲמָן הוּא יְבָרֵךְ אֶת בַּעַל הַבַּיִת הַזֶּה וְאֶת בַּעֲלַת הַבַּיִת הַזֶּה אוֹתָם וְאֶת בֵּיתָם וְאֶת זַרְעָם וְאֶת כָּל אֲשֶׁר לָהֶם. יְהִי רָצוֹן, שֶׁלֹּא יֵבוֹשׁ בַּעַל הַבַּיִת בָּעוֹלָם הַזֶּה וְלֹא יִכָּלֵם לָעוֹלָם הַבָּא, וְיִצְלַח מְאֹד בְּכָל נְכָסָיו וְיִהְיוּ נְכָסָיו וּנְכָסֵינוּ מֻצְלָחִים וּקְרוֹבִים לָעִיר וְאַל יִשְׁלַט שָׂטָן לֹא בְּמַעֲשֵׂי יָדָיו וְלֹא בְּמַעֲשֵׂי יָדֵינוּ וְאַל יִזְדַּקֵּק לֹא לְפָנָיו וְלֹא לְפָנֵינוּ שׁוּם דְּבַר הִרְהוּר חֵטְא וַעֲבֵרָה וְעָוֺן מֵעַתָּה וְעַד עוֹלָם.

### בראש חודש ובמועדים

אֱלֹהֵינוּ וֵאלֹהֵי אֲבוֹתֵינוּ יַעֲלֶה וְיָבֹא יַגִּיעַ יֵרָאֶה וְיֵרָצֶה יִשָּׁמַע יִפָּקֵד וְיִזָּכֵר זִכְרוֹנֵנוּ וְזִכְרוֹן אֲבוֹתֵינוּ זִכְרוֹן יְרוּשָׁלַיִם עִירָךְ וְזִכְרוֹן מָשִׁיחַ בֶּן דָּוִד עַבְדָּךְ וְזִכְרוֹן כָּל־עַמְּךָ בֵּית יִשְׂרָאֵל לְפָנֶיךָ לִפְלֵטָה לְטוֹבָה לְחֵן לְחֶסֶד וּלְרַחֲמִים לְחַיִּים וּלְשָׁלוֹם בְּיוֹם

בראש חודש: רֹאשׁ הַחֹדֶשׁ
בפסח: חַג הַמַּצּוֹת
בסוכות: חַג הַסֻּכּוֹת
בשמיני עצרת: שְׁמִינִי עֲצֶרֶת הַחַג
בשבועות: חַג הַשָּׁבוּעוֹת
בראש השנה: הַזִּכָּרוֹן הַזֶּה

זָכְרֵנוּ יְהֹוָה אֱלֹהֵינוּ בּוֹ לְטוֹבָה וּפָקְדֵנוּ בוֹ לִבְרָכָה וְהוֹשִׁיעֵנוּ בוֹ לְחַיִּים בִּדְבַר יְשׁוּעָה וְרַחֲמִים חוּס וְחָנֵּנוּ וְרַחֵם עָלֵינוּ וְהוֹשִׁיעֵנוּ כִּי אֵלֶיךָ עֵינֵינוּ כִּי אֵל מֶלֶךְ חַנּוּן וְרַחוּם אָתָּה.

**וּבְנֵה** יְרוּשָׁלַיִם עִיר הַקֹּדֶשׁ בִּמְהֵרָה בְיָמֵינוּ.
בָּרוּךְ אַתָּה יְיָ, בּוֹנֶה בְרַחֲמָיו יְרוּשָׁלָיִם. אָמֵן.

בָּרוּךְ אַתָּה יְיָ אֱלֹהֵינוּ מֶלֶךְ הָעוֹלָם הָאֵל אָבִינוּ מַלְכֵּנוּ אַדִּירֵנוּ בּוֹרְאֵנוּ גֹּאֲלֵנוּ יוֹצְרֵנוּ קְדוֹשֵׁנוּ קְדוֹשׁ יַעֲקֹב רוֹעֵנוּ יִשְׂרָאֵל הַמֶּלֶךְ הַטּוֹב וְהַמֵּטִיב לַכֹּל שֶׁבְּכָל יוֹם וָיוֹם הוּא הֵיטִיב הוּא מֵטִיב הוּא יֵיטִיב לָנוּ הוּא גְמָלָנוּ הוּא גוֹמְלֵנוּ הוּא יִגְמְלֵנוּ לָעַד לְחֵן וּלְחֶסֶד וּלְרַחֲמִים וּלְרֶוַח הַצָּלָה וְהַצְלָחָה בְּרָכָה וִישׁוּעָה נֶחָמָה פַּרְנָסָה וְכַלְכָּלָה וְרַחֲמִים וְחַיִּים וְשָׁלוֹם וְכָל טוֹב וּמִכָּל טוּב לְעוֹלָם אַל יְחַסְּרֵנוּ.

**וְעַל הַכֹּל** יְיָ אֱלֹהֵינוּ אֲנַחְנוּ מוֹדִים לָךְ וּמְבָרְכִים אוֹתָךְ יִתְבָּרַךְ שִׁמְךָ בְּפִי כָּל חַי תָּמִיד לְעוֹלָם וָעֶד כַּכָּתוּב: וְאָכַלְתָּ וְשָׂבָעְתָּ וּבֵרַכְתָּ אֶת יְיָ אֱלֹהֶיךָ עַל הָאָרֶץ הַטּוֹבָה אֲשֶׁר נָתַן לָךְ. בָּרוּךְ אַתָּה יְיָ, עַל הָאָרֶץ וְעַל הַמָּזוֹן.

**רַחֶם נָא** יְיָ אֱלֹהֵינוּ עַל יִשְׂרָאֵל עַמֶּךָ וְעַל יְרוּשָׁלַיִם עִירֶךָ, וְעַל צִיּוֹן מִשְׁכַּן כְּבוֹדֶךָ וְעַל מַלְכוּת בֵּית דָּוִד מְשִׁיחֶךָ וְעַל הַבַּיִת הַגָּדוֹל וְהַקָּדוֹשׁ שֶׁנִּקְרָא שִׁמְךָ עָלָיו. אֱלֹהֵינוּ אָבִינוּ רְעֵנוּ זוּנֵנוּ פַּרְנְסֵנוּ וְכַלְכְּלֵנוּ וְהַרְוִיחֵנוּ וְהַרְוַח לָנוּ יְיָ אֱלֹהֵינוּ מְהֵרָה מִכָּל צָרוֹתֵינוּ. וְנָא אַל תַּצְרִיכֵנוּ יְיָ אֱלֹהֵינוּ לֹא לִידֵי מַתְּנַת בָּשָׂר וָדָם וְלֹא לִידֵי הַלְוָאָתָם כִּי אִם לְיָדְךָ הַמְּלֵאָה הַפְּתוּחָה הַקְּדוֹשָׁה וְהָרְחָבָה שֶׁלֹּא נֵבוֹשׁ וְלֹא נִכָּלֵם לְעוֹלָם וָעֶד.

**בשבת קודש**

רְצֵה וְהַחֲלִיצֵנוּ יְיָ אֱלֹהֵינוּ בְּמִצְוֹתֶיךָ וּבְמִצְוַת יוֹם הַשְּׁבִיעִי הַשַּׁבָּת הַגָּדוֹל וְהַקָּדוֹשׁ הַזֶּה. כִּי יוֹם זֶה גָּדוֹל וְקָדוֹשׁ הוּא לְפָנֶיךָ לִשְׁבָּת בּוֹ וְלָנוּחַ בּוֹ בְּאַהֲבָה כְּמִצְוַת רְצוֹנֶךָ. וּבִרְצוֹנְךָ הָנִיחַ לָנוּ יְיָ אֱלֹהֵינוּ שֶׁלֹּא תְהֵא צָרָה וְיָגוֹן וַאֲנָחָה בְּיוֹם מְנוּחָתֵנוּ. וְהַרְאֵנוּ יְיָ אֱלֹהֵינוּ בְּנֶחָמַת צִיּוֹן עִירֶךָ וּבְבִנְיַן יְרוּשָׁלַיִם עִיר קָדְשֶׁךָ כִּי אַתָּה הוּא בַּעַל הַיְשׁוּעוֹת וּבַעַל הַנֶּחָמוֹת.

**בחנוכה ובפורים אומרים כאן על הניסים**
**עַל הַנִּסִּים** וְעַל הַפֻּרְקָן וְעַל הַגְּבוּרוֹת וְעַל הַתְּשׁוּעוֹת וְעַל הַנִּפְלָאוֹת וְעַל הַנֶּחָמוֹת שֶׁעָשִׂיתָ לַאֲבוֹתֵינוּ בַּיָּמִים הָהֵם בַּזְּמַן הַזֶּה.

לחנוכה

בִּימֵי מַתִּתְיָהוּ בֶּן יוֹחָנָן כֹּהֵן גָּדוֹל חַשְׁמוֹנַאי וּבָנָיו כְּשֶׁעָמְדָה מַלְכוּת יָוָן הָרְשָׁעָה עַל עַמְּךָ יִשְׂרָאֵל לְהַשְׁכִּיחָם מִתּוֹרָתָךְ וּלְהַעֲבִירָם מֵחֻקֵּי רְצוֹנֶךָ וְאַתָּה בְּרַחֲמֶיךָ הָרַבִּים עָמַדְתָּ לָהֶם בְּעֵת צָרָתָם רַבְתָּ אֶת רִיבָם דַּנְתָּ אֶת דִּינָם נָקַמְתָּ אֶת נִקְמָתָם מָסַרְתָּ גִּבּוֹרִים בְּיַד חַלָּשִׁים וְרַבִּים בְּיַד מְעַטִּים וּטְמֵאִים בְּיַד טְהוֹרִים וּרְשָׁעִים בְּיַד צַדִּיקִים וְזֵדִים בְּיַד עוֹסְקֵי תוֹרָתֶךָ וּלְךָ עָשִׂיתָ שֵׁם גָּדוֹל וְקָדוֹשׁ בְּעוֹלָמָךְ וּלְעַמְּךָ יִשְׂרָאֵל עָשִׂיתָ תְּשׁוּעָה גְדוֹלָה וּפֻרְקָן כְּהַיּוֹם הַזֶּה וְאַחַר כָּךְ בָּאוּ בָנֶיךָ לִדְבִיר בֵּיתֶךָ וּפִנּוּ אֶת הֵיכָלֶךָ וְטִהֲרוּ אֶת-מִקְדָּשֶׁךָ וְהִדְלִיקוּ נֵרוֹת בְּחַצְרוֹת קָדְשֶׁךָ וְקָבְעוּ שְׁמוֹנַת יְמֵי חֲנֻכָּה אֵלּוּ לְהוֹדוֹת וּלְהַלֵּל לְשִׁמְךָ הַגָּדוֹל.

לפורים

בִּימֵי מָרְדְּכַי וְאֶסְתֵּר בְּשׁוּשַׁן הַבִּירָה כְּשֶׁעָמַד עֲלֵיהֶם הָמָן הָרָשָׁע בִּקֵּשׁ לְהַשְׁמִיד לַהֲרוֹג וּלְאַבֵּד אֶת-כָּל-הַיְּהוּדִים מִנַּעַר וְעַד זָקֵן טַף וְנָשִׁים בְּיוֹם אֶחָד בִּשְׁלֹשָׁה עָשָׂר לְחֹדֶשׁ שְׁנֵים עָשָׂר הוּא חֹדֶשׁ אֲדָר וּשְׁלָלָם לָבוֹז וְאַתָּה בְּרַחֲמֶיךָ הָרַבִּים הֵפַרְתָּ אֶת עֲצָתוֹ וְקִלְקַלְתָּ אֶת מַחֲשַׁבְתּוֹ וַהֲשֵׁבוֹתָ-לּוֹ גְּמוּלוֹ בְּרֹאשׁוֹ וְתָלוּ אוֹתוֹ וְאֶת בָּנָיו עַל הָעֵץ וְעָשִׂיתָ עִמָּהֶם נִסִּים וְנִפְלָאוֹת וְנוֹדֶה לְשִׁמְךָ הַגָּדוֹל סֶלָה.

# BIRKAS HAMAZON

שִׁיר הַמַּעֲלוֹת בְּשׁוּב יְהוָה אֶת שִׁיבַת צִיּוֹן הָיִינוּ כְּחֹלְמִים. אָז יִמָּלֵא שְׂחוֹק פִּינוּ וּלְשׁוֹנֵנוּ רִנָּה אָז יֹאמְרוּ בַגּוֹיִם הִגְדִּיל יְהוָה לַעֲשׂוֹת עִם אֵלֶּה. הִגְדִּיל יְהוָה לַעֲשׂוֹת עִמָּנוּ הָיִינוּ שְׂמֵחִים. שׁוּבָה יְהוָה אֶת שְׁבִיתֵנוּ כַּאֲפִיקִים בַּנֶּגֶב. הַזֹּרְעִים בְּדִמְעָה בְּרִנָּה יִקְצֹרוּ. הָלוֹךְ יֵלֵךְ וּבָכֹה נֹשֵׂא מֶשֶׁךְ הַזָּרַע בֹּא יָבוֹא בְרִנָּה נֹשֵׂא אֲלֻמֹּתָיו.

שְׁלֹשָׁה שֶׁאָכְלוּ כְּאֶחָד חַיָּבִין לְזַמֵּן וְהַמְזַמֵּן פּוֹתֵחַ: רַבּוֹתַי, נְבָרֵךְ!
הַמְסֻבִּים עוֹנִים: יְהִי שֵׁם יְיָ מְבֹרָךְ מֵעַתָּה וְעַד עוֹלָם.
הַמְזַמֵּן אוֹמֵר: בִּרְשׁוּת מָרָנָן וְרַבָּנָן וְרַבּוֹתַי, נְבָרֵךְ (בעשרה: אֱלֹהֵינוּ) שֶׁאָכַלְנוּ מִשֶּׁלּוֹ.
הַמְסֻבִּים עוֹנִים: בָּרוּךְ (אֱלֹהֵינוּ) שֶׁאָכַלְנוּ מִשֶּׁלּוֹ וּבְטוּבוֹ חָיִינוּ.
הַמְזַמֵּן חוֹזֵר וְאוֹמֵר: בָּרוּךְ (אֱלֹהֵינוּ) שֶׁאָכַלְנוּ מִשֶּׁלּוֹ וּבְטוּבוֹ חָיִינוּ.

**בָּרוּךְ** אַתָּה יְהוָה אֱלֹהֵינוּ מֶלֶךְ הָעוֹלָם הַזָּן אֶת הָעוֹלָם כֻּלּוֹ בְּטוּבוֹ בְּחֵן בְּחֶסֶד וּבְרַחֲמִים הוּא נוֹתֵן לֶחֶם לְכָל-בָּשָׂר כִּי לְעוֹלָם חַסְדּוֹ וּבְטוּבוֹ הַגָּדוֹל תָּמִיד לֹא חָסַר לָנוּ וְאַל יֶחְסַר לָנוּ מָזוֹן לְעוֹלָם וָעֶד בַּעֲבוּר שְׁמוֹ הַגָּדוֹל כִּי הוּא אֵל זָן וּמְפַרְנֵס לַכֹּל וּמֵטִיב לַכֹּל וּמֵכִין מָזוֹן לְכָל-בְּרִיּוֹתָיו אֲשֶׁר בָּרָא בָּרוּךְ אַתָּה יְיָ הַזָּן אֶת הַכֹּל.

**נוֹדֶה** לְּךָ יְהוָה אֱלֹהֵינוּ עַל שֶׁהִנְחַלְתָּ לַאֲבוֹתֵינוּ אֶרֶץ חֶמְדָּה טוֹבָה וּרְחָבָה וְעַל שֶׁהוֹצֵאתָנוּ יְיָ אֱלֹהֵינוּ מֵאֶרֶץ מִצְרַיִם וּפְדִיתָנוּ מִבֵּית עֲבָדִים וְעַל בְּרִיתְךָ שֶׁחָתַמְתָּ בִּבְשָׂרֵנוּ וְעַל תּוֹרָתְךָ שֶׁלִּמַּדְתָּנוּ וְעַל חֻקֶּיךָ שֶׁהוֹדַעְתָּנוּ וְעַל חַיִּים חֵן וָחֶסֶד שֶׁחוֹנַנְתָּנוּ וְעַל אֲכִילַת מָזוֹן שָׁאַתָּה זָן וּמְפַרְנֵס אוֹתָנוּ תָּמִיד בְּכָל יוֹם וּבְכָל עֵת וּבְכָל שָׁעָה.

*Level 3 and Beyond!*

www.ingramcontent.com/pod-product-compliance
Lightning Source LLC
Chambersburg PA
CBHW071154070526
44584CB00019B/2791